ON THE EDGE

Your Catholic School Guide to Student Recruitment and Retention

by Daniel Horn

with contributions by
St. Genevieve High School students and staff

Copyright © 2013 Daniel Horn.

All rights reserved. No part of this book may be used or reproduced by any means, graphic, electronic, or mechanical, including photocopying, recording, taping or by any information storage retrieval system without the written permission of the publisher except in the case of brief quotations embodied in critical articles and reviews.

Balboa Press books may be ordered through booksellers or by contacting:

Balboa Press
A Division of Hay House
1663 Liberty Drive
Bloomington, IN 47403
www.balboapress.com
1-(877) 407-4847

Because of the dynamic nature of the Internet, any web addresses or links contained in this book may have changed since publication and may no longer be valid. The views expressed in this work are solely those of the author and do not necessarily reflect the views of the publisher, and the publisher hereby disclaims any responsibility for them.

The author of this book does not dispense medical advice or prescribe the use of any technique as a form of treatment for physical, emotional, or medical problems without the advice of a physician, either directly or indirectly. The intent of the author is only to offer information of a general nature to help you in your quest for emotional and spiritual well-being. In the event you use any of the information in this book for yourself, which is your constitutional right, the author and the publisher assume no responsibility for your actions.

Any people depicted in stock imagery provided by Thinkstock are models, and such images are being used for illustrative purposes only.
Certain stock imagery © Thinkstock.

Printed in the United States of America

ISBN: 978-1-4525-7023-5 (sc)
ISBN: 978-1-4525-7025-9 (e)
ISBN: 978-1-4525-7024-2 (hc)

Library of Congress Control Number: 2013904271

Balboa Press rev. date: 3/26/2013

With tremendous gratitude, I dedicate this book to:

Mr. Joseph Rawlinson and Mr. Kenneth Skinner

These two guys believed in St. Genevieve High School when few others did. Our school would not exist today if it had not been for them.

Contents

Acknowledgments ix
Foreword xi
Preface xiii

Chapter 1: When One Door Closes 1
Chapter 2: A Time For Reflection 11
Chapter 3: Creating the Ideal Catholic School
    Community: A Reflection 27
Chapter 4: Creating a Culture That Embraces Change 49
Chapter 5: Let's Meet 61
Chapter 6: Day-Caring 69
Chapter 7: Other Forms of Day Caring 75
Chapter 8: Themes to Live By 97
Chapter 9: Customer Service 109
Chapter 10: On the Road Again 123
Chapter 11: The Freshmen Retreat 129
Chapter 12: The Art of the Affirmation 139
Chapter 13: We Bow Before Thee 149
Chapter 14: Somebody Help Us! 169
Chapter 15: From the Edge of Despair to the Cutting
    Edge of Curriculum 177

Acknowledgments

I'd like to acknowledge the following people for helping to make this book a reality:

Father Alden Sison, for being one of the most supportive pastors and leaders out there.

Kathy Parker, for superb editing and for taking on the challenge of putting together all of the pieces — narrative, essays, and photos — into a cohesive book, of which we are all extremely proud.

Gabe Cheng, for supplying most of the photographs.

Howard Anderson, for a magnificent cover design.

Mary Bailey, for constant encouragement.

The National Catholic Education Association, for pointing me toward a new door.

Sister Clare Fitzgerald, for being an inspiration and friend to all of us at St. Genevieve.

The community of St. Thomas the Apostle School.

The students of St. Genevieve High School, for their enthusiasm and continual quest to be the best.

The faculty and staff of St. Genevieve High School, for making me so proud of them.

All the St. Genevieve students and staff who participated in the writing of this book, for sharing their perspectives.

Sister Mary Elizabeth Galt, for inspiring this book.

Foreword

Catholic school enrollment in the United States has continued to decline at an alarming rate over the past ten to fifteen years. The Archdiocese of Los Angeles realized that new strategies had to be identified to address this serious issue.

The response was to establish an aggressive marketing program engaging pastors, principals, faculties, and parents. While implementing the program, an area of serious concern that surfaced was the retention of students. Many schools experienced a growth in enrollment but within two to three years, a percentage of the original enrollment had declined. The questions arose: why were the schools not retaining those students, and what were the underlying causes for the lack of retention at the high school level? Thus, the reason for this book.

Mr. Dan Horn has been Principal at St. Genevieve High School for 14 years now. When he accepted this position, the high school was in a downward spiral. Within the first two years under his leadership, the school began to turn around. Not only did enrollment increase, the students were retained for all four years.

I approached Mr. Horn to address this critical topic at the April 2013 National Catholic Education Association meeting in Houston, Texas. Not only did Dan agree to speak at the meeting, he also decided to write a book addressing all aspects of the retention of students after realizing the importance of this topic. I am delighted with his response and look forward to this book being shared with a large audience of Catholic school leaders.

Sister Mary Elizabeth Galt
Chancellor, Archdiocese of Los Angeles
April, 2013

PREFACE

The Vibe

We recently opened a small café on campus. Before that, there was no food service at St. Genevieve High School, unless you count the catering truck that would appear twice each day attempting to meet our students' nutritional requirements. Students would often still be standing in line waiting to be served when the bell rang at the end of the break or lunch period, because they knew that once the truck left, there was nowhere else on campus to buy food, and they're never allowed to leave campus to satisfy a taco or burger craving (or for any other reason!) during school hours.

But even without offering adequate food service, we found that our enrollment was still on the rise. Apparently, it wasn't the food (or lack thereof) that attracted families to a particular school. In fact, we were able to reach our target enrollment before our café ever opened. Now that we do have a popular café, it's simply a bonus — some icing on the cake! — during our recruitment drives.

This year, we added a small, very modern lounge outside the café's serving area. We hired a graffiti artist to paint the walls, and in addition to your typical tables and chairs, we included outdoor lounge furniture for more casual dining. There are also two large flat-screen TVs. Students now congregate here before and after school to socialize and also to work together on class assignments.

The café is named The Vibe. Students suggested a variety of names, but The Vibe really summed up the energy you feel when you walk onto our campus.

The Vibe Café

There's a valuable lesson to be learned here. Think about it: for years we offered a lousy option for food — something that's actually pretty important to teenagers. Yet, our enrollment wasn't affected by it. While many Catholic school enrollments were trending down, ours not only went up, it surpassed our target. And only then did we get around to opening our campus café. Although it wasn't our café that brought more and more students to our campus, it was, in large measure, I believe, the overall "vibe" of our school that did increase our enrollment.

There's Just Something About This Place

There is a certain kind of energy here that just doesn't exist at a lot of schools. I can't tell you the number of visitors we've had on this campus who have all said largely the same thing. It usually begins something like this: "I've visited a lot of schools…"

When we hear these words, most of us know pretty much what is coming next, and it always brings a smile to our faces.

"...but I've never experienced a school quite like this one."

It's the vibe. We call it the Valiant Spirit. When I ask our students to define what that is, here is what they say:

Everybody here is nice and helpful!
It's fun being here!
The classes are fun, and the teachers are cool!
Everybody is respectful!
The teachers are helpful!
I love the way everybody treats each other!
Everyone is friendly!
St. Gen's doesn't lie when it says we are a school of character!
We don't judge each other!
The school spirit here is great!
People always greet me!
We're like family!
Teachers go out of their way to help you!
It's easy to make friends here!
Even upperclassmen are nice!
Students care for each other!
Teachers really understand where we're coming from!
It's like a second home!
People here are so kind!
I feel a part of something great!
Everybody cares about each other academically, emotionally, and spiritually!
It's an honest and caring environment!
My teachers continually inspire me!
There's an overall energy here!
Everyone is willing to help you with open arms!

These were actual written comments from seniors to freshmen, and represent the vast majority of those that were submitted. Yes, there were some about uniforms, theater arts, academics, sports, and even a few negative ones like "my mom makes me come here."

But by and large, students here are overwhelmingly positive. There's just something about the vibe of this school. It begins with a rather unique philosophy. And no, I'm not talking about the school's formal written philosophy statement, but rather, our daily vision to be a school of character.

There's An Attitude Here...It's Called Respect

Our café is kind of a symbol of who we are. We designed it to be a beautiful place of fellowship for our students. We want it to be theirs. We spent a lot of money building it and furnishing it. We ask them to respect it. This attitude of mutual respect is found not only in the café; we attempt to make our entire school beautiful, with inviting furniture and other nice things throughout.

Why do we bother? Well, we all spend a whole lot of time here. In many cases, we spend more waking hours on this campus than we do in our own homes. We wanted to create a warm and special environment. So, when you walk through our hallways, into our library, and even into our locker rooms, you'll see really nice things all along the way: leather chairs, pretty mirrors, nice lighting, fancy sofas. It has created a vibe of respect. We treat our campus with respect. We treat each other with respect. All the time? Of course not. Do our students make mistakes? You bet. So do we adults. That's partially what schools are designed for. However, by and large, there is an atmosphere of mutual respect on this campus that is hard to find in many other places today.

Creating a warm and special environment

Two Things to Remember

Throughout this book, you'll read a lot of stories and hear from a lot of people about successful recruitment and retention techniques, but in the end, everything boils down to two simple but important ideas:

1. You've got to have the right people in the right places.

2. Everybody wants to feel they matter (and, in fact, they do).

If you continue to keep these two key points in mind, they will keep you (and your school's enrollment) pointed in the right direction — upward.

Chapter 1: When One Door Closes

It may be an old adage, but that's because it's proven so often to be true: when one door closes, another opens. It is imperative during these challenging times in Catholic school history that we remain positive and focused on our goals.

Knowing ahead of time that we will inevitably face challenges and disappointments should prepare us to overcome these obstacles when they arise, and enable us to not give up too easily on achieving our goals.

A Secret to Happiness

One of the secrets to happiness as described in the book "The Four Agreements," by Don Miguel Ruiz, is "Don't Take Things Personally." It is a difficult goal to achieve for many of us who invest ourselves in such personal ways into the success of our schools. We often put in exceptionally long hours and sometimes sacrifice vacation time, holiday time, and even family time. It therefore becomes easy to associate what we *do* with who we *are*. That's a mistake. I learned that the hard way.

When I first became principal of St. Genevieve High School, I invested so much of my personal time in my job that I pretty much gave up exercise, was on a steady diet of fast-food, allowed my weight to balloon, couldn't sleep well, and became dissatisfied with how I looked and felt…sound familiar, anyone? Finally, after exactly six months on the job, my body shut me down — almost for good.

On New Year's Eve of 1999, instead of celebrating Y2K surrounded by family and friends, I was in an emergency room surrounded by medical staff who were attempting to save my life. After more than 20 days in the hospital suffering from a serious bout of pancreatitis, I emerged, wobbly and shaken, vowing to change my habits. Although my doctors believed I would not survive, God had opened another door for me, and I was determined to run through it.

I would change my habits. I would change my thinking. Had I died, it may have been a sad occasion for some, perhaps a relief for others, but the fact is, I would have been dead and all my crazy hours would have added up to zero, and by now my six month ministry at St. Genevieve High School would not even be a memory for most people. Balance. I needed to bring it back into my life.

When the Worst Thing Becomes the Best Thing

I can remember clearly the searing pain I felt on the morning of December 31, 1999. It is the worst physical pain I have ever experienced. Yet it turned out to be one of the best things that ever happened to me.

When I got out of the hospital, I was barely able to walk up a flight of stairs, having been bed-ridden and connected to tubes for almost a month. Once I learned that the diabetes I had acquired along with the onset of pancreatitis could have been prevented by proper diet and exercise, it got me to thinking: what kind of a message do we send students if we are only preparing them academically and socially for their futures? They might graduate from college, get high-paying jobs, drive the car of their dreams, and live in the big house on the hill, but what if they are not physically fit? My near-death experience had taught me a valuable lesson; it was a lesson I wished I had learned earlier, say, in high school or even grade school.

Exercise quickly became a regular part of not only *my* life, but also of the lives of all St. Genevieve High School students and staff members. The entire staff agreed during the spring of 2000 that we would implement an exercise program that fall requiring all students and staff to exercise at least three days a week, and preferably, four.

Getting Creative to Get Fit

We have limited space and facilities — only one gym and two locker rooms — so we had to get creative. We decided to pair up our teachers so there would always be two teachers working with a group of students. Since everyone would be exercising during the last period of the day, we didn't have the space nor the time to spare to have everyone change into exercise clothes. So instead, we changed our traditional Catholic school uniform to Adidas Wear. Students began wearing Adidas shorts and running pants with our school's newly designed Valiant t-shirts. Now, no one had to change from one set of clothes to another — the students were already dressed for exercise.

We began to see immediate results from our exercise program. One of the first — and most lasting — results is that when the final bell of the day rings, there is still high energy on campus. Exercise seems to rejuvenate students. Instead of the exhausted-looking faces we were accustomed to seeing, students were now leaving on an energy high. Some teachers, who decided to exercise along with the students, have expressed gratitude for providing them time to become more fit during their workday. And a number of students and teachers have reported dramatic weight losses since we began the program.

Exercise rejuvenates students

Over the years, there have been requests to replace the fitness classes with other classes or to use that time for other purposes. For the first three to four years, these requests were frequent; now, they are rare. We have established that the fitness class is something that is a priority here, and have offered students a variety of fitness class choices, including ballroom dancing, salsa dancing, hip-hop dancing, Pilates, yoga, hacky-sack, camp games, kickball, running, walking, biking, and more. When teaching candidates are interviewing, they know up front that if they are hired to teach math or science or whatever their subject area, they also automatically become a fitness teacher when hired.

Fitness For All

by Kerry Roche, English Teacher, St. Genevieve High School

The St. Genevieve fitness program offers a variety of activities — from walking, running, badminton, ultimate Frisbee, and group games to yoga, hacky sack, and the "Insanity" workout. Every student is required to take a class four days a week and all teachers pair up to lead a fitness class each quarter. Our school uniforms (track pants/shorts) are designed with fitness classes in mind, so students do not have to bother changing daily. Because the classes change quarterly, teachers and students are asked to be open  to new activities and to venture out of their comfort zone. Our program is unique and extremely beneficial to the St. Genevieve community in that it aligns with our holistic approach to education, which adheres to the philosophy that intellectual, mental, and physical health are all necessary for an individual's success.

During my interview at the school in 2007, I was told that all teachers were required to teach a fitness class.

I was skeptical at first. Though I like exercising, I am not an athlete, and I was also concerned that having to teach a fitness class would add to the already challenging workload. When I learned more about it, I realized it wasn't always about traditional exercise and athletics; instead, teachers were encouraged to teach a fitness class based on their own interests and experience.

After teaching a jazz/hip-hop class my first two years at St. Genevieve, I branched out to teach a variety of fitness classes. I now rotate between teaching boot camp, strength training, and yoga/Pilates. The students' involvement continues to surprise and delight me. When I was young, anyone who wasn't good at team sports hated P.E. class, so it is inspiring to see students who did little or no exercise getting better and challenging themselves to run that extra lap, or hold planks a little longer. Likewise, I still expect the majority of students to complain about the amount of physical work we do, especially in our 90+-degree valley heat, but for the most part, they have a great attitude, are always willing to work hard, and have a lot of fun doing it. The fitness program also provides an opportunity for teachers to connect with students in a more open environment, which often encourages them to do better back in the classroom.

When I started out teaching six academic classes and still had a seventh period of fitness, I feared not having enough energy for it all. In fact, the result was quite the opposite. Teaching fitness always energizes me for the rest of the day, and because I'm able to work out with the students, it's easy for me to stay fit despite my busy schedule. Also, during boot camp, I set aside time to discuss healthy eating habits, such as calorie intake and hydration, to make sure that students are not only getting enough nutrients to work out that day, but also know how to make healthy food choices in general. I currently teach a yoga/Pilates class that focuses not only on strength and toning, but also on the mind/body connection. This is one of my favorite parts of a hectic day! The fitness program has also motivated me to learn more about whatever class I'm teaching at the time, so I started taking several fitness classes myself in order to better educate my students on proper techniques and new exercises.

Students at St. Genevieve not only benefit from the fitness program, they really enjoy it, too. For example, juniors Edith Murillo and Andrea Rivera, students in my yoga class, commented that the class helped them relax at the end of a stressful day, yet was still "physically challenging." Edith said that she is "trying to do better every day." Senior Emanuel Marroquin likes the fact that fitness is mandatory for all four years at St. Genevieve, which is different from the traditional two-year California requirements. Senior Marilyn Gomez enjoys her group games class, saying that "it's fun" and that unlike at her previous school, no one is excluded from the teams and everyone here gets a fair chance.

St. Genevieve's fitness program clearly benefits both the staff and the students. In today's world, where there is so much emphasis on obesity and health issues related to a lack of physical activity, we can truly say we are helping one another develop healthy habits. With something as simple as thirty minutes a day, four days a week, we put away our electronic devices, interact with one another, and little by little, change ourselves and the world.

Sometimes You Have to Find the Door to Open Yourself

Recently, I knocked at the door (well, actually, it was a phone call) of the National Catholic Education Association. In the spring of 2010, the NCEA published "Living the Ascension," a short primer I wrote that offers some tips on effective marketing and recruiting. Since its publication, I've received a lot of positive feedback about the book, but also a lot of questions. I purposefully designed "Living the Ascension" to be a fast read, knowing that we educators don't typically have a lot of time. But I've discovered that while readers have appreciated the tips in the book, there appears to be an appetite to know more. Which is what brought me to the NCEA's door (well, conference call!) anew — I'd decided to approach them to pitch this new book.

Even though I think it was a pretty good pitch, I was told "no." The door was closed. However, prior to hanging up the phone, I realized I had just been done a favor. Right in front of me was the new door, which I would have never seen had the NCEA agreed to publish this book. By the time the call was over, I had made the decision to self-publish this book and to donate any proceeds to St. Genevieve High School. The door presented to me turned out to be my preferred choice — a choice I hadn't even realized I had.

You see, when they published my last work, the NCEA bought the rights from me. I received a nominal fee (which I accepted in copies of the book instead of dollars, knowing I'd be giving copies away). Also, the NCEA had edited out some important ideas that I thought should be included, so that the book could remain "politically correct." Now, having made the decision to self-publish, I could write exactly the book I wanted, without concern that ideas would be removed. Plus, there may even be a financial benefit for our school.

These days, so many of us are attempting to recruit families, build enrollment, and seek out dollars through donations, fundraising, and grants. With an economic drought over the past several years, the financial river has far less water than before and there are more of us fishing along the same banks. Add to that the financial challenges faced by the parents of our current and potential students, and the difficulties become increasingly complex. More and more families are requesting financial aid, those who were receiving financial aid before are requesting higher amounts, and many of our financial resources have either dwindled or disappeared altogether. In waiting for the economy to improve, I've gone from feeling like I had my finger in the dike to feeling like I need both arms up to hold the dam from crashing in on us.

It is easy to grow frustrated. It is easy to become overwhelmed by the "I want to give up" or "I can't do this anymore" feeling. However, if we are part of a team sharing the challenges, working together, while taking care of our own physical and mental health, it is easier to look for a new door when the one in front of us gets closed or even slammed shut.

So what do I hope you have learned from this chapter?

1. It is important to take care of yourself, both physically and mentally.

2. If you don't feel that you are part of a team, begin building the team.

Chapter 2: A Time For Reflection

Two books that helped me tremendously during the renaissance of St. Genevieve High School were "Good to Great," by Jim Collins, and "Raving Fans," by Ken Blanchard. We'll talk about "Raving Fans" in Chapter 9. For now, I want to briefly discuss "Good to Great."

In writing about corporate leaders who lead stunning transformations, Jim Collins wrote:

> The executives who ignited the transformations from good to great did not first figure out where to drive the bus and then get people to take it there. No, they *first* got the right people on the bus (and the wrong people off the bus) and *then* figured out where to drive it. They said, in essence, "Look, I don't really know where we should take this bus. But I know this much: If we get the right people on the bus, the right people in the right seats, and the wrong people off the bus, then we'll figure out how to take it someplace great."

One of the not so "politically correct" statements that was edited out of my last book is that there are people in education who should not be in education. There are teachers who should not be teachers, principals who should not be principals, pastors who should not be pastors, superintendents who should not be superintendents, and bishops who should not be bishops.

Canon law, which gives so much authority to our bishops and pastors, will most likely not be changing any time soon. Therefore, there is not much we can do if we have an ineffective bishop or pastor. However, when it comes to anyone else, change is somewhat easier.

Let's begin with ourselves.

Life-Changing Moments

by Jamie Chang, English Teacher, St. Genevieve High School

On May 17th, 2012, just two days before my wedding, I sat on the living room floor of my parents' house cutting strips of butcher paper. However, instead of the paper being a decorative project for my wedding, as one would assume, I was prepping for a job interview — the second of three I would have at St. Genevieve High School.

So many thoughts were spinning through my head as I tried to plan my lesson for the next morning. I kept hearing the person on the phone telling me to have a lesson ready for 25 remedial freshmen. I began to wonder, *who are these freshmen I was going to meet the next morning? Will my lesson be relevant to them? How will the classroom be set up?* As I thought about all this, I was excited but also somewhat anxious. Just a few minutes prior, my DJ for the wedding had called to say that he'd forgotten my wedding was this weekend! I felt like I was being pulled in different directions and questioned why I had even agreed to do the interview when I really should be trying to fix the wedding. However, something kept me going.

My first encounter with St. Genevieve High School is something I will never forget. As I entered the main building, a student walking down the hall greeted me immediately. At first I thought that this was some sort of fluke. Coming from an environment where students did not like to acknowledge their teachers in the hallway, I was surprised by the student's willingness to greet a total stranger. And it did not stop there. As I was directed to sit in a waiting area in the hallway, several staff members came to me to ask if I had been helped or if I would like some water. I began to see the nature that is St. Genevieve High School.

It is something that I'm somewhat reluctant to try to explain because, really, it is something that everyone should experience for themselves. I quickly learned that St. Genevieve High School does not "gloss" over the fact that they are a National School of Character; rather, they strive to live up to that title in their daily actions and relationships. Needless to say, it was refreshing to enter into such an environment and it intrigued me to want to learn more.

So I got my act together and arrived to do my lesson as planned. Yes, I was nervous, but once I started the lesson, the nerves seemed to fade away. I was reminded why I loved to teach and was able to block out the many adults whose numbers seemed to grow exponentially in the back of the room. After the lesson, I was ushered into a conference room, where the English department conducted a post-interview.

I was then introduced to three students from the class I had just taught, and *they* interviewed me as well. Having been through quite a few interviews, this was a definite twist that I hadn't expected. They were very professional, which was a bit surprising to me, since they were only freshmen. They were also very honest with their questions and asked me how much homework I would give and what I would do to help them prepare for tests. I chuckled to myself when they asked these questions, but appreciated that they genuinely wanted to know my answers. Although it certainly was different from anything I'd experienced before, I realized how thorough the interview process actually was. I left this interview knowing that I definitely wanted to be part of the St. Genevieve community, but unsure if they felt the same way.

Fast forward to less than a week later. I was sitting on the balcony of a hotel room in Kauai and heard my phone ring. I looked at the number and recognized it immediately. It's funny, looking back, how excited and nervous I was when I heard the voice at the other end. It was Maria Alvarez from St. Gen's, asking me to come in for a third interview. I immediately leapt out of my seat but tried to keep my voice level as we finished our conversation. We scheduled the interview for the day after I returned from my honeymoon.

I was nervous about having a one-on-one interview

with the principal whose face I only knew from visiting the school's website. As I walked up to the school's gate on the morning of the interview, Dan introduced himself. He was dressed casually and asked me about my trip to Hawaii, which immediately put me at ease. I had assumed this was both of our first times seeing each other, but Dan mentioned that he had been at my second interview observing, as well. During my interview with Dan, I got to learn more about the school's many unique qualities. I really appreciated this third interview because it felt like we were just two people trying to get to know each other outside the confines of a formal process.

In the end, I truly believe that God had a plan for me to be at St. Genevieve High School. He helped me manage to get through all the wedding drama and to meet amazing colleagues whom I continue to learn from every day. I feel blessed to be in a workplace that I can genuinely say pushes me to be a better person each day. When someone here opens a door for me or asks if someone needs help — and people at St. Gen's are doing things like this all the time — it reminds me that I need to do the same for others. I cannot say that everything is perfect at the school — we are human after all — but the staff definitely strives to model good character for our students, encouraging them to do the same for others. It is, I believe, our most unique quality among many positive qualities.

Mirror, Mirror

Years ago I noticed that some members of my elementary school staff were doing what I considered to be a lot of complaining about their peers. My staff knows how much I dislike hearing them complain about other staff members. My advice is always the same: Have you talked to that person about what is bothering you? Typically, the answer is "no." Then, I tell them, I don't want to hear about it. I am a problem solver at heart. When I hear there is a disagreement among staff members or that people have hurt feelings, I want to fix it. I never appreciate when people just want me to be as annoyed as they are by someone's behavior. Plus, it is not fair to that person, no matter what they've done, if they're getting complained about to the principal without them knowing. My policy is, if you bring it to me, I will not keep it to myself. If you will not say something, I will. Otherwise, keep it to yourself. If you won't do something about it, and won't allow me to intervene, then I don't want to hear about it.

However, the complaining continued. I had to do something. So I prepared a brief questionnaire with items such as:

What is this person's greatest flaw?

The one thing that annoys me most about this person is _____

If I could change one thing about this person it would be: ___

Give this person some sound advice that you know no one else is brave enough to offer.

Next, I called a faculty meeting. There was soft, meditative music playing as the staff walked in. A copy of the questionnaire was at each person's place, and people began to read the questions as they took their seats. I braced myself, and told the assembled group, "I'm about to have you draw a name from a basket. I'd like you to fill out the questions according to whose name you've drawn."

Immediately, glances were exchanged around the room in that "is this for real?" look of concern. "You will have ten minutes to fill out the questionnaire before turning it in," I continued. "So please take a few minutes now, look around the room, ponder what you might say, and think about how we can make this a constructive exercise."

Some hands instantly shot up. "I'll answer all of your questions in a few minutes," I said, "but right now, this is designed to be a time for reflection." During a somewhat uncomfortable silence for us all, I walked around the room with a basket from which each person drew a small piece of paper on which was printed, "Write in your own name."

There was a slight murmuring around the room as people realized that they were being asked to critique themselves, but when I asked if they had any questions, nobody did. "Please take the time allotted and fill out the questionnaire," I instructed.

When the ten minutes were up, I asked for volunteers to read their answers. Then I asked for people to share their feelings about the exercise. Most admitted a discomfort. One brave soul admitted having been looking forward to critiquing another person. In any case, I was able to make my point: we get so consumed by the faults of others that we don't provide the same kind of critical attention to ourselves. Once we do, however, we can then set about transforming ourselves into positive and happy individuals. And the more positive we are in life, the less we are bothered by the faults of others. It's a virtuous circle.

Renaissance

by Roxanne Brush, Religion Teacher, St. Genevieve High School

The ad in the paper mentioned being part of a "Renaissance" — my favorite time in history because it meant rebirth, a chance to start again, in a time when things were so dark and seemed to be hopeless. The Renaissance thinkers, inventors, and artists were not always recognized for what they were doing, especially in the beginning, but they were part of something bigger, something greater. I answered the ad in the paper because I was ready to start again, to go back to my Catholic roots and wherever they would take me; I wanted to be a part of this school's rebirth.

When I walked into St. Genevieve High School for my interview in July of 1999, the building looked as if it hadn't been touched since it opened in 1959. I couldn't find the entrance and when I finally did get inside, I noticed that the school was definitely lacking in many things. It also just seemed "dark."

But, after I met with Dan and John, the principal and vice principal, respectively, I walked out of the building knowing that I really wanted this job. There was something about them, the way they spoke about their hopes for the school and what was to come; I knew that this was the opportunity to fulfill my dream of being a teacher. Little did I know that I would experience so much more, and that the next thirteen years of my life would be both amazing and incredibly challenging.

Many new teachers were hired that year and we all seemed to be searching for our place among the veteran teachers, who were used to a particular type of leadership and for whom change was worse than any four-letter word you could think of. In the classrooms, none of the desks matched, tiles were falling off the ceiling, and the windows were obstructed. The faculty lounge had science experiments in the cupboards, uncomfortable seating, and if the walls could talk, it would probably be even worse than the gossip and negativity that was actually present in that room. There was a battle over how much paper you would receive to make copies, and the purchasing process had to change in order to cut costs.

With no official training or materials, I was supposed to teach ESL in a shared classroom. Because I had some public relations experience, I also became the alumni director, development director, the cheer coach, and was asked to help with admissions and recruitment. Of course, being new, I took on whatever was asked of me. Like the Renaissance thinkers, though, it was going to take a lot of trial and error, and we "newbies" would be the ones to fight the uphill battle. But the fact is, I wanted to do whatever I could to make this school great.

I learned a lot that first year — and in each of the following thirteen years, as well. We have come a long way, but it has taken a lot of patience, time, and the support of many people at the school, whom I consider to be my second family. Every year is different, and each one is a new opportunity to make the most of that amazing word called change. Here are ten "lessons" I've learned along the way of what is really an ongoing renaissance:

1. Never give up believing what you know is right. If you believe in the school and believe it is your calling, stay there — it will get better because *you* will make it better.

2. Stay positive despite all naysayers and disbelievers. Resist the urge to be negative yourself. During our first WASC accreditation, there was so much negativity in the room you could cut it with a knife. When I suggested changing the name of the process to create a more positive view of it, I was publically ridiculed by a veteran teacher. I will never forget the way that made me feel. It would have been so much easier to fall in line with the "dark side," but I just couldn't do it. Positivity, I realized, is one of my gifts, and I'm grateful for that.

3. Be helpful and do your best to live out the mission, but know that you can say no, especially when you already are doing so much. Saying no is not a bad thing, but figure out why you are saying no. Is it because you are resisting change or because you are overwhelmed? If it is the latter, see #6 below and do not assume that others will turn you down.

4. To quote Rick Warren, "It's not about you." It's about the kids. And after the kids, it's about the parents, and

then the alumni. Then it's about the administration and your coworkers. After that, maybe it is about you and "your" classroom. If you make it about you, you lose, and so does the school. If you make it about everyone being interconnected, you win ten times over.

5. Self-evaluate every week. The only person you can control is yourself. Evaluate your lessons — what's worked and what hasn't. Evaluate your ability to contribute in helpful ways like assisting a colleague or sending positive emails to parents.

6. Invite others to share and to help. Whether it's sharing your ideas or making time to socialize, you learn when you give and receive. People — whether parents, alumni, or coworkers — want to be "invited" to do something. So ask, especially when you need help. A personal invitation can make all the difference.

7. Search for free resources and make sure to share those, too. I am always amazed by the people who teach kids in Third World countries, where there are 80 kids to a class, no desks, and maybe three books. No Internet, no crayons, no paper. The teachers teach with music and with stories and by being good role models. I don't remember much from my own high school experience, but I will never forget the teachers who were "real" and who exemplified the kind of person I wanted to become.

8. We teach kids, not just subjects, so you should love what you teach. If you lose that love, find it, or at the very least, reevaluate it and find out where you belong.

9. Whatever benefits you have, know that they will be doubled when an alum tells you that you inspired him

or her to be the doctor they've now become. Or a student shares a story with you and you realize that you're the one who planted that seed, which just took time to grow. These are the true benefits of what we do. Celebrate these moments.

10. Get involved and say yes to opportunities and taking chances that may involve any or all of the above. The time and effort you put in will be worth it. Change can be scary, but when you truly believe in the future, one change may be all it takes for great success. Often, the only real change that needs to be made is in our attitude.

The Renaissance didn't happen overnight. It began with one idea that inspired others, and all of those ideas became part of one another. People realized that together, a community can move mountains; that's what we have done at St. Genevieve High School, and you can do it, too.

Moving On

How do we know when it is time for us to move on to another school or perhaps to another career? What we do as educators has such an effect on the future of our world that it simply is not fair for the burned out, the angry, the negative, or the bitter to remain in the field.

When I was in elementary school back in the early 1970s, I felt cursed to have a science teacher who was, in my opinion, mentally ill. She was verbally and physically cruel to students she perceived to be misbehaving. Yet even though she made us — even the "good" kids — spend an entire year in fear during science class, we somehow had convinced ourselves that she was a "good" teacher. "We sure learn a lot in her class," we would find it comforting to say to one another. The fact is, decades later, I don't remember a damned thing that lunatic taught us! What I do remember is her pride in mistreating her students. What I think about now is, where were the other adults in the school who knew first-hand that this teacher was abusive? Why didn't they do something?

This case is extreme, and that particular teacher probably had a mental illness. Hopefully, a teacher like her could not exist in today's classrooms. But what about the ineffective, the inefficient, the apathetic, or the uncooperative ones? Or the ones who don't even like kids and obviously don't like the profession. Why are *they* still teaching? What are they still doing in the classrooms of the 21st century?

The fact is, if we have teachers in our schools who should not be teaching, or at the very least need a jumpstart, then it is the responsibility of someone in a leadership position to do something about it. Why should we expect families to pay tuition if there is a teacher, a principal, or even an aide or a coach, who is not top-notch?

In my own archdiocese, which has hundreds of schools, I have observed several cases where the pastor, for various reasons, has allowed a principal to bring a school to its knees. When even parents whose children are comfortable, have friends, and feel safe, begin pulling their kids out of school, you have to seriously question what's going on. When families start pulling their kids out of a school, they are usually willing to talk. In many cases, they've already been talking, but no one was listening. So why aren't we listening? Why do so many pastors wait until a school is almost to the point of no return before making the tough decisions? I ask that rhetorically since I know that the answers can vary widely.

Pastors, Are You Listening?

Pastors, this is a wake-up call to you. If your school's enrollment is decreasing, you need to look carefully at your school's leadership. Just because someone is a good teacher or a nice person does not mean they will make an effective principal. When it becomes obvious that someone needs to be replaced, we have a tendency to say, "but s/he is such a nice person." A friend of mine has a saying, "the nice guy's club is full." It is a reminder that we are in the business of educating children, not of providing jobs for nice people.

Of course it is difficult to fire someone or ask someone to resign. It should be a last resort after we have had the difficult conversations, suggested clear changes to be made, and provided needed guidance. When the required changes don't take place, however, or perhaps are happening too slowly, then it is time to straighten your backbone and make the hard call. I have witnessed far too many pastors who use the excuse of being "pastoral," when in fact, they are not considering the greater good of the entire flock — only the sheep in charge. You must be pastoral with a spine, and make the call for the greater good of the school and parish.

If you are a pastor of a school in trouble: have you seriously considered a change in leadership? If you have, what kind of interviews are you conducting? Just because a principal is successful at one school does not guarantee success in turning another school around and increasing its enrollment. Are you looking specifically for someone who has either been successful in building enrollment or who has outstanding ideas about how to do it?

Does your parish want a school in the future? There's an interesting question. Perhaps you don't. Why not? Maybe you don't know enough about your existing parish school. Why don't you? Is there nothing to know? Perhaps you do know, but don't like what you're hearing. My school, St. Genevieve, is a parish high school. But back in 1999, most of the parish didn't seem to know there was still a parish high school in existence, while most of those who did were not pleased about what they were hearing.

Whose responsibility is it to change things? I believe it is the responsibility of the pastor. Why aren't there good things being published weekly in your parish bulletin? Why aren't you, as the pastor, bragging weekly about your school? If you have nothing to brag about, it's your own fault. As the pastor, you should be demanding bragging rights from your principal. During an average school week, there should be plenty of good news about the school to publish in the bulletin to entice parishioners to consider enrolling.

Any Bishops Out There Reading This?

Bishops, the same message I just gave to the pastors is also true for you. If you have a school with declining enrollment in your diocese, take a look at the pastor. These days, while the bench is admittedly thinner than it once was, if we continue to value Catholic education, then we still need pastors who are committed to the cause and can make the tough calls on leadership in their parish schools. We need pastors who are not only willing to support the school, but are committed to helping the parish school thrive.

Recently, in our diocese, a relatively newly ordained priest was placed in a parish where the school had a rapidly dwindling enrollment. Although there were priests who were older and more experienced, this priest of only four years was named administrator because he had previously been a Catholic school teacher and vice-principal. Whoever made this decision was on top of things. Here was a new administrator who obviously had a love for Catholic education. In short order, that school, St. Gertrude the Great, has begun to show important signs of a renaissance.

Calling All Principals

Have you convinced yourself that the reason for your school's decline in enrollment is the changing neighborhood? The demographics? The national trend in Catholic schools? If so, stop for a moment and look within. As hard as it may be to hold that mirror up, you need to do it. Right now. Perhaps, instead of finding someone who is not meant for the game, you may find someone who really is ready to take on the challenge of creating a community of change. Perhaps you will find someone who may not have done a quite good enough job as of yet, but is now ready to accept the gauntlet.

These are matters of integrity. A teacher I now have a great deal of respect for was a former teacher on my staff, whom I did not respect at the time. Even though this person was the negative sort, who rarely saw anything positive in anything the administration did, it still bothered me that I had such little regard for a staff member. After a year of constant complaining, the teacher resigned and accepted a job in another school. Interestingly, this final act was what began to earn the teacher some respect from me, as I think it takes integrity to realize that you may not be the right fit for a particular place. And who knows, that next school might be exactly the right fit. I admire the fact that rather than continuing to do nothing but complain, this person made the choice to move on to a situation that was, hopefully, a better fit.

This is your moment of truth. Do you have enough integrity to complete some intense self-reflection to determine if your current setting is the right fit for you?

Chapter 3: Creating the Ideal Catholic School Community: A Reflection

I encourage you to have every member of your school staff complete the reflection provided in this chapter. If you are a pastor or teacher, take a copy of this book to your school's principal. If you are the principal, make sure that all of your teachers — and YOU — complete this reflection!

Have you ever proofread something you've written and missed an obvious mistake? Yes, we've all done that. Sometimes our brains are programmed to see what we want to see. There are times when we see the correct spelling and punctuation when a glaring mistake is staring right at us. Could this also be true with the spirit and the intent we bring to our ministries? For many people, the answer is yes. The real question, however, is: are you willing to take a hard and honest look at yourself, your attitude, and your contributions to your current school community, and then make the necessary changes to help your school grow? Do you have the integrity to admit where you have possibly failed or where your weaknesses are, as well as to applaud yourself for the areas in which you excel? It is important to do both; it does not help to become shy and humble — let your light shine!

If you really want to have people do the following reflection honestly, have people discuss their answers at a faculty meeting. If anyone on staff is reluctant to participate, or if you are developing a knot in your stomach just imagining having this type of a discussion, it is most likely a sign that you should be paying attention to. If you, as principal, are too uncomfortable leading this discussion, is there someone on staff who can be trusted to lead what can be a delicate and sometimes emotional conversation? Or is there someone you can bring in from the outside to deftly lead an honest conversation among everyone?

If in the end, the staff is far too uncomfortable to have a group conversation, consider having the conversation between each teacher and your principal. One way or another, it has to be decided whether your particular group of staff includes the right people in the right places at this time in your school's history. This exercise is intended to begin that conversation.

If your staff is willing to participate in the reflection exercise and truly have a serious discussion, make certain to put some ground-rules in place prior to having the discussion:

First, everyone must participate.

Honesty is essential.

The end-goal must be growth as a staff.

One person speaks at a time.

Everyone must speak in a tone that is respectful.

Whoever feels that the tone is becoming too negative, loud, or unproductive has a responsibility to call a time out.

Everyone promises to actively listen to what is being said, rather than simply waiting his or her turn to speak.

Now, let's begin…

In April of 2000, I created an intensive self-reflection for the members of our faculty that afforded me an opportunity to articulate a vision for our staff and put us on a course that eventually led us to our current situation: a model of an ideal Catholic school community!

This particular set of questions worked for us at that particular time in our school's history. One of the implications of the questionnaire — which took most people between five and eight hours to complete — was that if you wanted to remain on our staff, you were going to have to work hard. If staff members decided they were not going to return, they could simply indicate that and were spared the time of filling out the questionnaire. However, filling out the questionnaire did not assure anyone of being offered a contract. I read each and every answer, wrote comments throughout each booklet, and had individual conversations with every staff member. After some of those conversations, it was decided that not everyone was ready to go in the same direction I was.

Obviously, this exact set of questions will not necessarily be right for your specific situation. But if you use it well, it should prove to be as groundbreaking a moment in the history of your school and staff development as it was in ours. What I suggest is that together as a staff, you decide how many and which questions are right for you. Simply having this first discussion about which questions to include will begin your process of staff reflection. Once you have determined the questions, allow adequate time for each member of the staff to respond. Decide if the conversation is between the principal and individual teachers, or if you dare, have a conversation with the entire staff.

Ladies and gentlemen, I now present: **Creating the Ideal Catholic School Community**. Our journey in this quest began with this letter:

April 2, 2000

Dear Faculty,

I'd like to see the first line of our school's philosophy read, *"Saint Genevieve High School is an ideal Catholic School Community."* This one sentence very well sums up my vision and my hope for our school. I don't know if it's possible to achieve an *"ideal"* Catholic school community, but I believe that philosophy should serve as a compass, which is constantly referred to in order to insure we are headed in the right direction. So why not head in the direction toward ideal?

More than anything, I want our school to become a daily, living, breathing, Christian experience for all who pass through our doors. I want for us to become a quintessential Catholic school, one in which a high degree of love and respect is evident from the moment a student applies to the day they receive their diploma. I want for the spiritual lives and direction of ourselves, our colleagues, and our students to be the first and foremost priority. Students will learn more about Christian living from teachers who give love, offer cooperation, and show tolerance than they will from four years of religion classes. They will be more inclined to love and lead Catholic/Christian lives when they have witnessed teachers who view themselves as ministers and spiritual directors. And they will achieve more academically, athletically, and personally when their self-esteem and spirit are a top priority nurtured by their teachers and coaches.

Most schools, especially Catholic schools, like to say "we're like a family." In certain respects that is a true statement for every school. After all, in many cases, students spend more waking hours with their classmates, teachers, and coaches than they do with family members. And school communities, like families, are subject to dysfunction. Dysfunction results when relationships are not valued; therefore, people don't work at them. For any relationship to succeed, it takes effort. I've done a great deal of observing since I arrived in July. At times during this academic year, I have sometimes observed more effort put into gossip, hearsay, and negativity than into attempts at effective communication. This must change.

Let's face it: St. Genevieve High School is not for everyone. The disagreements that took place this year were too frequent and at times downright unpleasant. I told you in November I was spending 75% of my time resolving conflicts among staff members, and the percentage has remained about the same. I have no intention of investing that kind of time on the same issue next year. You've heard the saying "a house divided cannot stand." From what I've observed, there have been entirely too many divisive comments made, and too many divisive conversations had. Today, we begin healing our house and mending any divisions.

I'm requiring each of you who are interested in returning next year, as well as those who are undecided, to participate in what should prove to be an intensive reflection and self-evaluation. The goal of this exercise is to provide you with what I hope will be insight into the future for our school and community. Up to now there have been too few who have stepped forward to help move our school forward. At times I've seen teachers set higher standards for students than they were willing to reach themselves. Although we complain about parents and students who offer excuses rather than accept responsibility, I continue to marvel at the excuses I hear from teachers rather than acceptance of reasonability. In the future, more will be required of St. Genevieve teachers, not less.

If I receive your response indicating a desire to have your contract renewed, I will trust you have carefully read and reflected on the pages following. Note that the questions are designed not only to assist you in evaluating your performance this year, but they serve as a framework or compass for where we are going. I expect that each person who requests to have their contract renewed understand that every member of our staff in the coming year will be expected to be actively involved in creating the *Ideal Catholic School Community*. This will require additional efforts in and out of the classroom. It will require that each staff member share in the leadership of our school through your help in establishing a parent organization as well as taking part in the planning of the faculty retreat. It will require a team spirit from all of us. Too often I have witnessed the same people routinely volunteering to help with additional responsibilities such as Mardi Gras, or serving on an admissions committee, etc. A progressive future for our school will depend upon people who can and are willing to be involved in all aspects of school life.

In the pages that follow you will find descriptors of the ideal Catholic school educator. The evaluative questions will provide you with additional insight as to what will be expected of St. Genevieve faculty in the future. Some of you have already met the criteria; some have even exceeded it. However, some have not contributed their fair share to the overall school environment. Some, through negative thinking and comments, have held back our progress. This process should help both of us decide whether you should be commended for your efforts this year, if you need to have a change of heart, or if you need to resign.

This evaluation will be due on April 17th at 8:00 a.m. or earlier. Make certain to answer all questions that are relevant to your present position. Prior to May 15th I will meet, for analysis, with each faculty member who is undecided or wishing to return. I've also extended an invitation to Monsignor Chris to join in these meetings. On or prior to May 15th you will receive notification as to whether or not a contract will be offered for the 2000-2001 school year.

Sincerely,

Dan Horn

P.S. Please write your answers on these pages. If you need additional space, use the reverse side of the paper.

Then, there was an intent form, which read like this:

This is NOT an offer of a contract or contract renewal.

It is simply to provide you with the opportunity to indicate your interest in renewing your contract for the 2000-2001 school year. If you are presently undecided or desire to renew your contract please read thoroughly the Descriptors of the Ideal Catholic School Educator and complete the evaluation pages that follow. The evaluation is due on or before April 17th. Prior to May 15th I will meet with each person who is undecided or wishing to renew. We will discuss your evaluation and prospects for returning. On or before May 15th you will receive notification as to whether your contract will be renewed.

If you have already decided that you will not be returning, simply note that on this form, sign it, and return. There is no need to complete the self-evaluation.

_____ I would like to renew my contract for the 2000-2001 school year.

_____ I am undecided about my intent to renew.

_____ I will not be returning for the 2000-2001 school year.

Print Your Name					Sign Your Name

Date

The next three pages outlined descriptors of the Ideal Catholic School Educator. They read as follows:

Descriptors of the Ideal Catholic School Educator

(Derived from Church documents on education received as part of a graduate education class at the University of San Francisco)

The ideal Catholic school teacher, a community builder...

- Contributes to a school atmosphere of respect and cordiality
- Forms "persons-in-community"
- Participates in the school's shared vision
- Respects the tradition of the Catholic Church
- Affirms the dignity of each student
- Nurtures student diversity
- Cultivates a global consciousness
- Is socially and ecologically aware, locally, nationally, internationally
- Teaches to peace and justice issues
- Establishes rapport with students
- Develops caring student relationships
- Exercises prudence in student relationships
- Values dialogue with students
- Is an active listener
- Is psychologically present to students
- Possesses patience and humility
- Collaborates with colleagues
- Is a team player
- Builds "authentic" relationships with colleagues

- Collaborates with parents
- Creates parent partnerships based on faith
- Acknowledges parents as primary educators
- Assists the education of parents
- Integrates service into the curriculum
- Creates community outreach opportunities for students
- Belongs to Catholic and secular professional education organizations
- Creates outreach opportunities with other schools, Catholic as well as other private and public schools

The ideal Catholic school teacher, committed to lifelong professional development...

- Maintains awareness of the latest advances in teaching methodologies, in psychology, and in the world at large
- Is passionate to improve and expand his or her teaching methods
- Is continually ready to renew and adapt the curriculum
- Collaborates with the secular educational community
- Is an innovator
- Understands that constant and accelerated change characterizes our age and affects every aspect of life
- Envisions new forms of schooling that may more appropriately meet the needs of students
- Experiments in judicious ways to improve educational effectiveness

- Engages in cooperative teaching opportunities with colleagues

The ideal Catholic school teacher, committed to lifelong spiritual growth...

- Views himself or herself as a minister
- Possesses a vocation to Catholic education
- Possesses special qualities of mind and heart
- Models a moral lifestyle and character
- Models Christ's message
- Possesses a love for, and understanding of, today's youth
- Appreciates the real problems and difficulties of people
- Is committed to the progress of the apostolate of Catholic education
- Is able to put Christian ideals into practice
- Daily witnesses Christian values to students
- Is committed to student formation
- Is faith-filled
- Understands Catholic doctrine
- Incorporates pedagogy that emphasizes direct and personal contact with students
- Inspires the education community with his or her spirituality
- Views his or her role in the Catholic schools as an apostolic mission
- Understands Catholic doctrine
- Possesses background in theology, ethics, and philosophy
- Is aware of the social teachings of the church

- Celebrates Christian values through the sacraments
- Displays harmonious interpersonal relationships
- Consistently puts forth effort to be available to students
- Understands that professional competence in the Catholic school includes the commitment to ongoing personal spiritual formation
- Engages in periodic self-evaluation on the authenticity of his or her vocation to Catholic education

And finally, the set of 30 questions, most of which required a narrative response:

1. An ideal Catholic school teacher teaches to peace and justice issues. What were your feelings in devoting the opening week of school to the Lessons Learned From Columbine? How do you feel about incorporating more of the same kind of activities into our curriculum?

2. Write about your proudest moment in the classroom this year.

3. Describe the best or one of the best lessons you taught this year.

4. Other than sense of humor, what do you think students would say they like best about you?

5. What do you think students would say if asked to provide an adjective describing the teaching and learning in your classroom this year?

6. How would students describe the general environment in your classroom? Are students respectful of you? Their peers? Is it conducive to learning? Would

students agree that you have control of the class? Rate overall level of respect presented in your classroom.

Excellent Good Average Below Average Failure

7. Would students say that you are impartial or that you have favorites?

8. How would you describe your teaching style? What percentage of time is spent on lecture, discussion, textbook, questioning, research, hands-on activities? Do you make an effort to vary your style to appeal to the multiple intelligences of students? If yes, how? Rate your ability and willingness to vary your teaching style.

Excellent Good Average Below Average Failure

9. Other than test and quizzes, what opportunities have you provided for students to indicate their level of learning and growth?
Rate your overall ability and willingness to use alternative forms of assessment.

Excellent Good Average Below Average Failure

10. Have any of your classes taken any field trips? Have your classes utilized the library? What about guest speakers?
Rate your use of opportunities and resources outside the classroom used to enhance the learning process.

Excellent Good Average Below Average Failure

11. Estimate what percentage of your questioning of students requires critical or creative thinking. Rate your variation of questioning.

Excellent Good Average Below Average Failure

12. What efforts do you make to involve every student in the learning process? Would all students say they feel as though they are valued members of your class? Rate your involvement of all students and your ability to make them feel valued.

    Excellent Good Average Below Average Failure

13. What is your planning process? Where do you normally do your planning? How much time per week do you spend? How far in advance do you plan? Is your planbook up-to-date?
    Rate the overall effectiveness of your planning.

    Excellent Good Average Below Average Failure

14. What is your approach to discipline? Would students say your goal is to mete out punishment or to change behavior?
    Rate your effectiveness in maintaining discipline.

    Excellent Good Average Below Average Failure

15. An ideal Catholic school teacher is a team player. Describe your contributions to creating a team environment. Do you volunteer to help other staff members? Do others see you as someone they can approach for assistance for long- or short-term projects? Do you enjoy working with others, and do others enjoy working with you? Are you collaborative? Do others feel comfortable sharing their opinions with you? Do others feel comfortable to disagree with you?
    Rate yourself as a team player.

    Excellent Good Average Below Average Failure

How do you think others would rate you as a team player?

    Excellent Good Average Below Average Failure

16. When you disagree with another staff member, how do you handle it? Are your disagreements with staff ever discussed with students?
Rate your handling of disagreements.

   Excellent Good Average Below Average Failure

17. Gossip and hearsay can be the downfall of any community. How do you handle gossip and hearsay?
Rate your handling of gossip and hearsay.

   Excellent Good Average Below Average Failure

---

17) Gossip and hearsay can be a downfall for any community. How do you handle gossip and hearsay?

Unfortunately, our world thrives on it but you can choose to believe it or not. You can choose to pass it on or block it out or stop it. I try to handle it by not spreading it. There always been tidbits and at times its hard to block out. But I am the one who chooses to believe it and I try not to get involved. It happens though and I believe I still have to learn more about doing my part to stop it. Lord help me to do so and to go to the horses mouth with questions or concerns.

Better to discourage it before _____.
Sooner or later you know who has _____ good vs poor intentions in their conversations. Why participate — only listening — Encourage gossip.

Rate your handling of gossip and hearsay.
Excellent (Good) Average Below average Failure

18) For next Spring I am tentatively planning a three-day two-night faculty retreat. Write about your interest and ability to attend. What value would there be in such a venture for you personally and for us as a staff? Would you be interested in being part of the leadership team in planning that retreat?

That would be FABULOUS! Vegas? (Just kidding) I would love to have a retreat that would be longer than a day. It would allow so much more time for bonding and learning — with each other and with ourselves. It is all to easy to get caught up in every day life and sometimes we all need to get away — for more than a couple of hours.

18. For next spring I am tentatively planning a three-day, two-night faculty retreat. Write about your interest and ability to attend. What value would there be in such a venture for you personally and for us as a staff? Would you be interested in being part of the leadership team in planning that retreat?

19. For a school to continually improve there must be time for adequate planning and meetings for staff, departments, committees, etc. Have you made our staff meetings this year a priority? Do you see the value in additional meeting time? Would you be willing to help in planning and executing a staff meeting?

20. Describe the daily prayer experiences in your classroom this year. Write about the frequency, who led them, what the reaction was from students. Judging from students' reactions, do you think they found the experience of prayer in your classroom meaningful?
Overall, how would you rate the prayer experience provided by your students?

    Excellent Good Average Below Average Failure

21. In an ideal Catholic school community, students, teachers, and coaches feel as though their work in and out of the classroom is appreciated. Write about your support for fellow teachers, coaches, moderators, and students. Did you attend athletic events, the student play, Mardi Gras, mock trial or any other after-school or weekend events? Write about any support or assistance you provided. Overall, how would you rate your support of extracurricular activities other than those you moderate or coach?

Excellent Good Average Below Average Failure

How do you rate your overall support of colleagues?

Excellent Good Average Below Average Failure

How do you rate your overall support of students?

Excellent Good Average Below Average Failure

22. Tell about your attendance this year. How many days have you missed for illness, personal reasons, meetings, workshops, etc? Were the number of days missed and reasons fair to you, your students, and colleagues?
Rate your attendance for the year.

Excellent Good Average Below Average Failure

23. Write about your punctuality. Do you arrive on time to school, for your classes, for faculty meetings, club meetings, athletic practices, games, etc?
Rate your punctuality.

Excellent Good Average Below Average Failure

24. Describe your grading habits and punctuality in returning students' work. Are you timely with your results to students? How long is your average wait period for students to receive work or tests back? Describe the feedback you provide for students.
Rate your punctuality in returning student work.

Excellent Good Average Below Average Failure

25. How have you participated in the WASC process this year? Have you actively contributed during meetings? Have you been positive or negative about the process? Are you contributing your fair share to the project?

Rate your overall contribution to the WASC process.

Excellent Good Average Below Average Failure

Rate your overall punctuality in meeting deadlines for turning in exams, grades, etc.

Excellent Good Average Below Average Failure

26. An ideal Catholic school teacher integrates service into the curriculum. Describe any opportunities or engagement offered students regarding service projects. What is your interest level in helping to plan a service project with students? What is your interest level in participating in a service project with students?

27. An ideal Catholic school teacher collaborates with parents. What is your interest level and availability in helping to form and to be active in a parent-teacher-student partnership? (aka PTA, PTO, PTG). Describe what you envision your role being in such an endeavor. Would you be able to take an active role in the leadership and formation of such a group?

28. Other than classroom teacher, list any other responsibility you've had, for instance coach, club moderator, recruitment, department chair, etc. Write about your overall effectiveness in that leadership role. What were some of the lessons that students or colleagues were able to learn from the way you executed your role?

29. What leadership role do you envision for yourself in helping our school to achieve that Ideal Catholic School Community?

30. If you are invited to return for the 2000-2001 school

year, what would be your top three goals? Describe how each will help to establish the Ideal Catholic School Community.

Yes, it was an exhausting process for us all. However, it changed the course of our interactions. It would take years before I was able to look my staff squarely in the eye and say with all sincerity, "This is the best staff I have ever worked with!" But the journey was well worth it, and it all began with this exercise.

Good luck on your journey!

Rethinking Titles

by Patrick Palmeter, Assistant Principal, Dean of Character Formation, St. Genevieve High School

In the spring of 2000, my principal, Dan Horn, offered me the position of Assistant Principal, Dean of Discipline. As I contemplated the offer, I could not help but reflect on a quote by Dr. Martin Luther King: "Education is not enough. Intelligence plus character — that is the true goal of education."

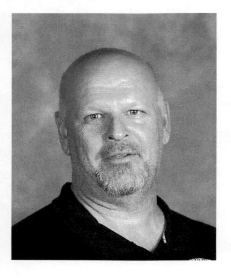

I enjoy teaching and building relationships with students on a daily basis, and, consequently, was somewhat reluctant to take a position outside the classroom. At the time, our school was at a crossroads, and Mr. Horn was determined to "change the view" of St. Genevieve High School by changing what was happening on the inside. Mr. Horn wanted to build an ideal Catholic school community where academics were important but where graduating good human beings was equally as important. I wanted to play a part in the true education of our students. So after some reflection, I agreed to take the position; however, I had one condition.

I did not like the title of Dean of Discipline and wanted to change it to Dean of Character Formation.

The school had many handbook policies regarding uniform and appearance that seemed silly; students felt scrutinized and student morale and pride were at a low ebb. Students' attitudes toward the Dean and toward discipline were very negative. We needed to rethink discipline and I wanted to focus my attention on the issue of building character rather than on what students were wearing.

I believe that the goal of discipline should be to change behavior and enhance moral development, and should not be solely rooted in consequences and punishment. My role as Dean is guided by a principle of education writer Alfie Kohn's, that good teaching is less about doing things *to* kids and more about working *with* them. Students also need to learn to accept the consequences for their decisions, but more importantly, they need to reflect and grow morally from them, which is why I felt the change to my title was necessary and appropriate.

As Pope Pius XI said, "Hope springs eternal in the hearts of teachers that each student will learn how to make decisions as one who thinks, judges, and asks constantly and consistently in accordance with the right reason illumined by the supernatural light of the example and teaching of Christ."

Chapter 4: Creating a Culture That Embraces Change

Change scares people. Does change require us to be brave? To have courage? Not really. We don't need courage to face change so much as we need it to have the necessary conversations with those who have grown mired in standing still.

Ever heard of Stockholm Syndrome?

Stockholm Syndrome describes the behavior of kidnap victims who, over time, become sympathetic to their captors. The name derives from a 1973 hostage incident in Stockholm, Sweden. At the end of six days of captivity in a bank, several kidnap victims actually resisted rescue attempts, and afterwards refused to testify against their captors.

This syndrome, I believe, can be adapted to many other situations in life if we are not careful. For example, people can become so afraid of change that even if the outcome will be good for them, they often choose to stay with what they know simply because it is what they are comfortable with.

Moving Forward vs. Staying Put

Living in the information age has caused many of us educators to realize that our schools have stood still for far too long. While we are preparing our students for jobs that may not have been invented yet, we still cling to certain ideas and methods that, in many cases, are no longer working. Why?

One reason is because it's difficult to have forward-thinking conversations with people who react out of fear, people who, rather than thoughtfully considering — and possibly trying out — new ideas when they are presented to them, instead often dig in their heels or become loud, stubborn, and unreasonable.

Trust me. I have had more than my share of these kinds of conversations with teachers and staff over the years. For instance, during my first weeks at St. Genevieve High School, I decided that no textbooks would be used and there would be no formal academic classes. For most of the staff, these were rather untraditional ideas. So was changing the dress code to allow any length or color of hair. Come to think of it, when I wanted to have classes on Saturdays or Sundays for the first time, it caused some serious wrinkles in many (most!) people's thinking. Same thing happened when I proposed having night school several times throughout the year. Take the entire school on a field trip to the Hollywood Bowl? Every teacher teach an exercise class? Do an overnight faculty retreat to Mexico? Add 15 days onto the school calendar? Start school in July? Have classes on Good Friday? The list goes on, but I think you're probably getting the idea.

Field trip to the Hollywood Bowl? Yes!

The key is, I understand paradigm change. I also understand that when those in your community understand paradigm change, it helps a whole lot in being able to actually *implement* change. And when they don't, the opposite is true…watch out!

School on Saturday? How to Change a Paradigm

While I am far from being an expert in developmental psychology, I have been at the forefront of implementing some rather major changes at the two schools where I have been principal, and have had rather impressive results at both. So pardon me for simplifying Piaget, but here is my explanation for how a paradigm is changed.

It begins with a new idea, which often causes disequilibrium or the feeling of being uncertain or off-balance. School on a Saturday? I've never experienced that before! Granted, it is a strange idea, and those hearing it for the first time typically want to fight against it to regain their feeling of balance. They begin to list all of the perceived reasons why having school on a Saturday cannot work. Now comes the time for patience and even a bit of courage, depending on how hostile one's audience becomes. But when people know ahead of time that disequilibrium is part of the change process, it allows ideas to stay in the ballpark (for a while, at least), rather than being immediately tossed out like a foul ball.

The second step is assimilation. This involves an ongoing conversation, not only with the person who proposed the idea (in this case, me!), but with other stakeholders as well. This is where those opposed have the opportunity to raise all their doubts, while I, as the idea-holder, get to reinforce the rationale for my idea. "Well, if we are having our annual Open House on Saturday since that is when most people can come," I say to the doubters, "doesn't it make sense that our visitors actually get to see our classes in session?"

During the assimilation period, issues may be raised that I hadn't previously considered, so I need time to walk away for further contemplation. The others, too, need time to walk away and sit with the new idea for a while. Usually, during this period, as they have the opportunity to talk with other stakeholders, people begin to see that the new idea might actually have some merit.

There is always give and take in these discussions. School on a Saturday does not have to be a full 8:00 a.m.-to-3:00 p.m. kind of a deal. What is our real purpose? Our purpose is to have classes going on while we have Open House visitors. Open House is not going to last all day. It can be an abbreviated kind of a day.

What are the benefits of people seeing school actually in session? There are many. One of the most obvious is that it will lead to us having a larger freshmen class next academic year, won't it? Well, won't it? If not, then we have some other issues we need to deal with first. But if we have the right people in the right places, then of course we want our visitors to see our school in action.

As time goes by, what began as a ludicrous-sounding idea to many, begins to make sense. Most of us are here for Open House anyway. Now we just have to get the students here. Why shouldn't the students play an important role in the legacy of their school? Why shouldn't they and their parents be a part of this important — and historic— conversation?

The final step in the paradigm change is accommodation. People begin to accommodate to the idea of having school on a Saturday; it begins to seem like a smart thing to do. They begin to own it.

Resist Your Resistance to Change!

by John Van Grinsven, Math Teacher, St. Genevieve High School

You might think that being on the wrong side of needed change — change that was proposed to the administrative team by the newly hired principal in a time of crisis — would mark me as the next educator out the door (especially in a failing school, as ours was at that time), but in this case, you would be wrong. I had, in fact, been blessed with the opportunity to grow from my resistance to change. My participation in the administrative team meetings and the resulting decisions and events turned out to be life changing for me. Because of that struggle, I became a better educator and a better person, someone who now actually welcomes change as a daily lesson that many others often fail to see or understand. I was fortunate to have a principal who still believed in me, even though I was initially resistant to the changes he proposed.

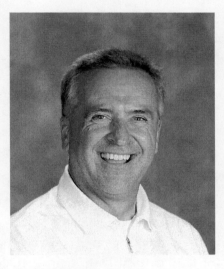

When I began my teaching career in 1980, it was back at the Catholic high school I graduated from, which, at the time, had a great reputation in the community. Unfortunately, during the 1990's the school failed to meet the needs of its students and it began a decade-long spiral into decline. The school's reputation became so bad that the student population declined each year, from over 1100 in the 1980's to only about 300 in 1999. In 1997, I accepted the role of vice principal of academics, hoping to be able to reverse some of the negative trends. I knew that changes were needed to revive the school, but I was not prepared for the depth and breadth of the changes that were required.

For the 1999-2000 school year, new principal Dan Horn accepted the challenge of leading the rejuvenation of the failing St. Genevieve High School. In August, Dan called together the administrative team for the most important meeting the school had ever undertaken; our discussions and the forthcoming decisions would lead our school either to its eventual death or its renaissance.

We urgently needed a strategic plan that could revive our deteriorating school. Little did I know how my resistance to what lay ahead was going to alter my attitude to change, and challenge my whole understanding of how to deal with it. In that decisive administrative leadership team meeting, I was respectfully resistant to our principal's opening-week-of-school plan. His idea focused on creating a new school culture featuring a yearly theme, which would require eliminating all our "normal" first-week activities. I couldn't imagine the first week of school with no time for academics; no discussions of course syllabi, books, or supplies; and no time afforded to teachers to introduce their courses. I begged and pleaded with the new principal for a minimal amount of time — even five minutes per class — to be carved out of the opening week's schedule for academics. But when the final decision was made to have no academic time this opening week, I quickly realized that I was on the wrong side of coming change.

My mind was spinning. How would our students — and our school — improve if academics were not one of the main points of emphasis for the opening week? Could this untested plan really bring about the necessary changes to ensure our future? And if so, how?

I had so many concerns and doubts (I now refer to this as my doubting Thomas impersonation period). I was also worried that Dan may have lost faith in me as his vice principal due to my resistance to his strategic plan. During the subsequent planning meetings prior to the opening of school that year, Dan continued to clarify his vision. He began to really put my mind at ease when he graciously offered me the opportunity (he still believed in me!) to become directly involved in developing the specific procedures for orchestrating this groundbreaking plan and altering the direction of our failing school. Dan's personal invitation for me to help with the planning process — his response to my resistance — was pure genius. His reaching out, and the cooperative nature of the planning sessions that followed, went a long way to bridging any perceived divide and built new roads of trust among us all.

As it turned out, Dan's proposed direction of change was the miracle remedy needed to resuscitate our struggling, small Catholic high school. The course of action I initially resisted led to a complete renaissance of the school, which, in fairly short order, earned the distinction of becoming the first Catholic high school recognized nationally as a School of Character. Student and teacher morale improved. The student population doubled. Today, the nurturing, self-sustaining school culture is noticed by all who visit the campus and still continues to improve some thirteen years later. Not only is St. Genevieve High School more successful now than it's ever been before, it also has made me a better person, educator, and leader. I am proud of the school's accomplishments, and of my own.

Surprise! Change Can Be Fun

Once the community makes a major change, such as the one described, and it reaps a successful result — and a "successful" result can vary depending on how you define it — it becomes far easier to implement future changes.

Other ways to create a culture that embraces change? Show some TED Talks videos at faculty meetings, or screen Joel Barker's great video on changing paradigms. Have the entire staff read and discuss articles about change. Do simple things such as challenging people to sit somewhere other than in their normal seat at a faculty meeting or in the faculty lounge. Serve something new at the annual faculty luncheon or go somewhere other than the regular standby place that "everyone likes." Change the location of your faculty meetings. Don't always have the same person leading prayer. Surprise everyone by doing something they won't expect.

Note: The first time I suggested that our entire school attend a performance at the Hollywood Bowl, I almost faced a mutiny. We recently took more than 700 people on our 13th annual trip there, and it was, as always, a highlight of the school year for us all!

Playing by Ear: Growing a High School Music Program

by Carlos Dominguez, Band and Orchestra Director, St. Genevieve High School

In 2008, while I was substitute teaching in Hawthorne, California, I ran across an ad for a music teacher at a small school in the San Fernando Valley. Until that moment, I had never given much thought to being a music teacher. My goal was to make a living as a professional musician. But, at a time when gigs were hard to come by, I decided to give this new and different opportunity a try. What followed was one of the greatest opportunities to come my way, and, I believe, the greatest opportunity that could have been given to any new music teacher.

When I came to St. Genevieve High School in October 2008, the music program was barely a year old. The marching band consisted of 24 students, many of whom were about to graduate. Over the next five years, the band would eventually swell to 57 members. Today, approximately 100 students are enrolled in one or more music classes. Students have the choice of Beginning Orchestra or Band, Marching Band, Advanced Orchestra, and Jazz Band.

Passion and patience are the keys to success in any program, but especially in a music program. The teacher must have a passion for music as well as for teaching. The teacher's passion can be passed on to the students, but it will take time for many parts of the program to come together. It took five years, in fact, before our student musicians were able to begin competing and going to festivals. Before that, I was spending most of my energy simply establishing a culture of music at the school.

Perhaps the greatest part of coming to St. Genevieve High School as a young band director was having the opportunity to try out different musical ideas to see what would work. But the growth and success of the music program has really been made possible because everyone in the St. Genevieve community — from the administration to the students to the parents — has been involved each step of the way. Today, our principal, teachers, students, and parents regularly attend a variety of band and orchestra performances.

Being the band director at St. Genevieve High School has truly been an amazing and fulfilling experience for me as both a teacher and an artist. I've not only seen our music students grow and thrive, I've also seen our entire school community transformed by the many benefits offered by our increasingly vibrant music program.

The St. Genevieve H.S. Marching Band

Chapter 5: Let's Meet

Meetings? Look at all your scheduled meetings for the year. Now consider this: just because it's the first Friday or second Tuesday of the month is not enough of a reason for a meeting. On the flip side, just because your school has only had faculty and staff meetings once a month in the past does not mean that once a month will suffice in the future.

I have a policy: I try to be respectful of people's time when it comes to meetings. Personally, I think we're in an age that makes it necessary to have more meetings than ever before. With all the additional demands on teachers, and in order to adapt to ever-changing curriculum opportunities, I sometimes think that having a daily built-in meeting time would be ideal. But thanks to technology, our meetings can be smarter and more effective. The days of calling a meeting just to go over the week's events should be well gone. Put it in an email!

Meetings of Substance

Bring people together for reasons of substance. If you are reading this book, chances are that your school is looking for ways to have a thriving future. Therefore, it is even more important than ever that your meeting time be put to good use.

Unless you have brought someone in to conduct an in-service, I believe that meeting time should involve conversation among staff members. You should be talking about issues that are relevant to growth: curriculum, parental involvement, staff development, etc. After a visit to another school, have staff members present a report or lead a discussion. Provide time for teachers to plan cross-curricular lessons or to ensure vertical alignment within departments.

Spiritual Development

Part of my strategy in building morale is to devote faculty meeting time to matters of the spirit. These days when almost all of us are so incredibly busy, it takes a brave leader to call people together for the simple purpose of prayer, meditation, or expressing gratitude. However, that brave leader will very quickly be rewarded for his or her intention. Although people will sometimes act resentful about having taken up valuable time that could have been spent "getting things done," most rational people will be thankful and grateful for those rare opportunities to slow down and have their spirit nurtured.

Just Plain Fun

Meetings don't all have to be serious. I've taken our staff to the movies, miniature golfing, and most recently, when the Space Shuttle Endeavor was flying atop a 747 around Los Angeles, we happened to be having a staff development day. So I rented a bus, put everyone on board, and we went to a garage rooftop in Hollywood to experience a once-in-a-lifetime moment together as Endeavor circled above. At the conclusion of the 2011-12 school year, we all took the TMZ tour of Hollywood, and then had lunch together on the Sunset Strip prior to breaking at the end of the semester. By getting together as a group and making lasting memories together, we build bonds that, in the long run, benefit not just ourselves, but contribute to the success of our students and our school.

Faculty field trip to view the Space Shuttle Endeavor

An In-Depth Interview Process

by Dr. Michelle Hunter, Science Department Chair, Biology Teacher, St. Genevieve High School

The St. Genevieve High School staff consists of highly motivated individuals who have a deep passion for their subjects and are extremely focused on creating a cutting-edge learning environment that develops the interests — and spirit — of our students. The faculty is extremely collaborative and, in fact, interacts as a "family," challenging one another to consistently grow and develop as people and educators. The establishment and maintenance of this unique culture is ultimately contingent on the caliber of each faculty and staff member. So how do you identify individuals who are going to enrich the culture of the school while rec-  ognizing those who would be detrimental? It all starts with the extensive and effective interview process at St. Genevieve High School.

I experienced this process firsthand in May of 2011. I was excited to interview at St. Genevieve because of their mission statement and how involved their faculty members are in so many different activities. I wanted to find a work environment that would provide many opportunities to challenge myself and foster my diverse set of interests. When I entered the school for my interview, I was immediately welcomed by students and staff members who shook my hand and asked if I needed help. The facilities were immaculate and everyone I encountered seemed energetic and extremely happy. I remember being so impressed by the culture of the school, which I could already feel, even before my interview began!

My first interview started with basic questions regarding my experience and teaching philosophy. The interviewing panel consisted of the Principal, Vice Principal of Academics, Dean of Character, and one of the Academic Counselors. I had the impression that they were trying to get a sense of who I was and why I was interested in teaching. The panel and I had specific discussions regarding how I felt about being a Campus Minister and if I was Catholic. They described their liturgies and let me know what my role would be in these events. They listed different retreats that occur during the year and asked if I would be interested and available to participate. They discussed the school schedule and asked about my ability to adapt to it. They described several hypothetical scenarios involving students and parents, and asked how I would respond to them. The interview panel was candid about the philosophy of the school, the unique schedule, and the demands placed on the staff, and they fully answered all of my questions. At the conclusion of the interview, the panel made it clear that I should take some time to really determine whether I would thrive in this type of work environment, because it is not for everyone; they then invited me to return for the second interview. I left feeling as if I had a clear picture of what the experience would be like as an educator at St. Genevieve High School.

While the first interview painted a picture of the school overall, the second interview allowed me to experience what it would be like to actually teach there. I was invited back to teach a lesson to a class of students and was given information regarding the content that the students were covering so that I could design my lesson to fit into their current unit of study. I was there for the first period of the day, and experienced the school-wide prayer, pledge, and morning announcements. Several department members and administrators arrived to observe me teach. Being able to teach the students directly was the most informative part of the interview process. Here I had a group of students that I could directly interact with to assess their interest in the subject matter, their prior knowledge, their pace, and what kind of learners they were. I specifically designed my lesson to not only demonstrate my teaching style, but also to collect as much information as I could about this representative population of students with whom I would potentially be working. The information I gathered was invaluable.

After teaching the lesson, I returned to the conference room with a group of five or six students. This focus group of students interviewed me, while I, in turn, interviewed them. I was incredibly impressed by the students' demeanor and quality of questions. I knew I was interacting with a unique group of students and they were doing something really cutting-edge at this school. Next, I met with a department member who discussed department-specific information while further reiterating the time demands and flexibility required for success at St. Genevieve High School.

This concluded the extensive interview process. As a candidate, I now had a clear picture of the priorities and expectations of the school. I had the ability to experience what it would be like to actually teach there and what the students were like. The process allowed me to determine whether St. Genevieve High School would be a good fit for me when thinking about my professional goals. I was able to accept the job offer with great confidence knowing that this was the perfect environment for me, a place where I could flourish and challenge myself.

At the end of my first year teaching, a position opened up in my department and I was asked to be the department representative during the interview process. So I now had the opportunity to interact with the interview process from the other side of the table — as part of the interview panel.

During the first interview, we gauged the experience and demeanor of the candidate. There was candid dialog regarding the philosophy and expectations of the school. After the applicant exited, the interview panel compiled a general list of strengths and concerns that had arisen during our time with the candidate. This gave us some key focus points to look for during the teaching demonstration, which, once again for me, was the most informative part of the interview process. Observing the lesson in the classroom immediately established the candidate's experience, teaching philosophy, and behavior-management style. Additionally, we could see firsthand how the students were responding to the candidate

— were they engaged, interested, learning? After the interview process concluded, I recorded my impressions and opinions as did the other panel members.

With extensive time spent together and comprehensive information gathered — both in and out of the classroom — this in-depth interview process enables both the administration and the applicants to make truly informed decisions about who will and will not be a good fit for our school.

Chapter 6: Day-Caring

If yours is an elementary school, I will assume that you offer daycare. If not, you should begin to immediately explore the possibility of doing so. Few parents these days have the luxury of being able to drop off and pick up their children at the school's regular opening and closing hours. Do parents — and your school — the favor of implementing a daycare option that meets the scheduling and financial needs of the majority of your parents.

When I became an elementary school principal, the school already had an outsourced daycare program in place. Although it was a convenient offering for the school, it was not especially convenient — or affordable — for many of our parents. When I discovered that a large number of our families were taking advantage of a daycare program being provided by the city park next door, I initiated our own program.

Our program offered several advantages both for the school and our families. First of all, since I was hiring the employees, I could set the hours, which meant we could easily adapt to the specific needs of our families all year long — even throughout the summer, when we became the first elementary school in the archdiocese to have a 195-day school year. The days that fell between Memorial Day and Labor Day concluded at 12:30 p.m. In order to provide a solid academic day, there were no extras — no art, no physical education, no electives or music — until we went back to full days after Labor Day. This allowed for both teachers and students to feel as though there was a much lighter load during the summer months, and even the teachers were able to leave by 1:00 p.m. three days a week. However, for parents who needed it, there was daycare.

Worth the Trip

by Joshua Hernandez, Student, St. Genevieve High School

"Joshua, hey Joshua, it is five o'clock! Time to wake up for school!" Every time my mom wakes me with these words, I joyfully get out of bed and get ready to start my day. I think about my friends and teachers as I get ready to go on my adventure. I call every day of school an adventure because of the long trip I take to get there and back. Every morning at six o'clock I take a one-hour bus ride just to get to school.

My family and friends always ask me, "Why do you go to school so far away from your house?" I just look at them and shrug because I'm never sure how to answer their question. So I thought, maybe if I write about it, I'll come up with the answer.

When I arrive at St. Genevieve I start to get a feeling of pure excitement in my stomach. I think about all of the possibilities that the day holds for me and all that the school has to offer. I jump off the school bus and walk onto the St. Genevieve campus. Every morning as I make my way to zero period I can't seem to make it to class without my friends stopping me and wanting to say hi or embrace me. It is because of these people that my day is so worthwhile. My friends from other schools always talk about bullies, and about how their teachers are strict and unfair. When they ask me about my school experience, I always have positive things to say about St. Genevieve.

St. Genevieve is an outstanding place. It is my second home and sometimes it's even hard for me to go home because I just love the atmosphere of the school so much. I probably spend more time at St. Genevieve than at my own home, but I'm not bothered by that because I consider my friends and teachers my family, too. I can go to them for anything I ever need. It's usually hard for me to talk to people on a personal level but with all the trust and love I feel from each person at St. Genevieve, I have no difficulty speaking my mind with them.

St. Genevieve provides students with so many opportunities and programs, that I have become far more involved in school than I thought I would ever be. I have participated in Band, Drumline, Track and Field, Film Club, Tech Club, and Journalism. Drumline is my favorite. It feels great performing with people who share your common interest — and then bringing home first-place trophies in drumline competitions. In addition to extracurricular activities, I have also been in an AP class, made honor roll, participated in events like Masses and homecoming, and even met former President Jimmy Carter. Not many high school students can say they hosted a former United States president.

I can't express how much this school means to me. My life will forever be modeled after the six pillars of character that I've learned about here. St. Genevieve sets a high bar, which I believe that other high schools should try to reach.

Getting up at five o'clock to sit on a school bus for an hour isn't so bad when it takes you to a place where you are surrounded by people who care about you. I now know how to answer the question my family and friends always ask me. I go to St. Genevieve because it has a campus full of students and teachers who actually care about me and want the best for me. Plus, the school offers me new opportunities every day. I will always be proud of being a Valiant at St. Genevieve. It is more than just a school; it is a gateway for great things to come. Other teachers and principals should look to St. Genevieve if they want to know how to run a high school right.

Creative Calendaring

Since we were now going to school all 12 months of the year, I thought it necessary to adjust the calendar so that there was always some kind of a break to look forward to. For instance, I did my best to ensure that we were never in school for more than three solid weeks without then having a long weekend. We also took a week off in the fall as well as our Easter week vacation. We also had some extra-long weekends throughout the year to keep everyone motivated. I found that teachers tend to love taking that fall break. It's not only less expensive to travel during that time of year, it's also typically less crowded and the weather is usually excellent around the country and in other places in the world where teachers can enjoy their break.

Profiting from Daycare

Of course, for our working parents, we continued to offer affordable daycare year round. And because our daycare program was so affordable, so many of our families took advantage of it that, beyond the many benefits it provided, the school actually ended up making a profit from our popular daycare program.

Chapter 7: Other Forms of Day Caring

Elementary schools should offer good daycare programs. But *all* schools should provide many forms of what I call "day caring." Smart schools will find a number of ways to involve their students in caring and effective programs and activities while they are on the school's campus, even — or especially — if it's before or after their regularly scheduled class time. Here are a few examples.

Study Halls and Tutoring. When we extended our school year at St. Genevieve High School to 195 days, we eliminated our summer school. We now have a five-week summer break, and yes, we are back in session by the end of July. But when we adopted the additional 15 days of classes, we did so with the goal of ensuring that no students will fail — not to make teachers or students attend summer classes. We do offer supplemental online class work for students in Advanced Placement classes during the summer. During the academic year, we try to meet as many needs as possible, and put enough safety nets in place to secure the success of each and every student. If a coach has scheduled practice at a time that conflicts with our tutoring program, the grade-level counselor has the authority to hire additional tutors and to work out a mutually agreeable time to tutor the team.

Extended Library Hours. Most days, the St. Genevieve library is open for 12 hours, from 7:00 a.m. to 7:00 p.m. It's a quiet and comfortable place for students to read, do research, or use the library's computers to complete assignments.

Campus Café. Ever since the recent addition of our campus café, The Vibe, it's become a popular place for students to eat, socialize, and make plans at various times throughout the day. It helps that the café is open from 7:00 a.m. to 6:00 p.m.

"What can we get you?" At The Vibe Café

Caring Faculty. When we've asked students what they like about their teachers at St. Gen's, they've readily replied that teachers "will answer our questions," "explain things so we can understand them," "don't get mad if we need to have things explained several times," "invite us to come in before or after school if we don't understand something," and "spend time helping us." Do students at your school say similar things about your teachers? You won't know if you don't ask.

Theater Arts. When I was principal at St. Thomas elementary school, a young college student dropped by one day and said she wanted to volunteer some hours by teaching dance classes. I paired her up with our kindergarten teacher, who had been a Broadway actor, and within a year, Mt. St. Mary's College was lending us their theater space and we were bussing our entire school of inner-city youngsters to a college campus to see their peers perform in "Annie." In fairly short order — though it took a lot of effort and volunteer hours — we had a wonderful theater arts program, which continues to this day, more than two decades later! I took my own love of musical theater with me to St. Genevieve High School, when I became principal there. Prior to 1999, there was very little music to be heard at St. Gen's. When we discovered that our community enjoyed attending — and performing in — musical theater, I began budgeting for two musicals a year. Now, 80-plus students are involved in staging musical theater performances twice a year, which has helped to transform not only our school but our entire community, which is a sizable — and very appreciative — part of our audience.

Theater of Dreams

by Nain E. DoPorto, English Teacher and Musicals Director, St. Genevieve High School

"If you build it, they will come." Ray Kinsella, played by Kevin Costner in the film "Field of Dreams," is seen having heard this whispered to him from his cornfield, when suddenly a baseball diamond materializes in front of him. It was this moment of cosmic intervention that would inspire Ray to build a baseball field in hopes of reuniting the lost players of a famous local team, and ultimately, his treasured family.

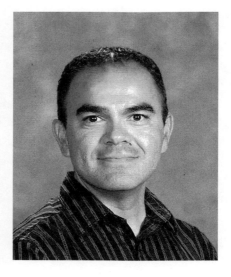

This is somewhat akin to what it was like for me when Principal Dan Horn, then in his third year with St. Genevieve High School, traversed the school grounds and finished his personal tour with me at Madonna Hall, the venue where the school would house all of its future theater productions. Despite all limitations, by raising the framework of a strong theatre arts program, by feeding it and by nourishing it for the benefit of all of Panorama City in the hope of fostering a budding creative community, people would recognize something special that they would want to be a part of.

Some dozen years ago, Mr. Horn had a vision for St. Genevieve, which, at the time, was a troubled school with falling enrollment and little enthusiasm for things scholastic or extracurricular. He worked at strengthening the rigors of academics and brought in a team of like-minded educators to help fashion a school that would bridge these invigorated academics with the arts and athletics to help build a holistic program for the student-learner.

Like the Costner character in "Field of Dreams," I immediately saw the potential that Madonna Hall held for our school's future theatrical endeavors: black draperies materialized along the walls, an extension to our small stage space grew in front of our feet, piping was erected above and around us to help embellish future sets with backdrops. My own vision of St. Genevieve's Theatre Arts Program was encouraged by an instant enthusiasm and passion for the arts by the school's growing faculty, staff, and student body.

Our show selections were carefully decided upon by Mr. Horn, the choreographer, the vocal director, the music director, and me. We carefully looked at the current pool of talented St. Genevieve students and considered what a particular show could do to inspire future performers. The school began to transform from having little love of theatre, with seniors who felt entitled to all the lead roles, into a supportive community eager for the next big show and a student body who was learning the lesson that "there are no small roles, only small actors." The playing field was leveled, with roles thrown open to all students, which meant that we have subsequently seen freshmen, sophomores, juniors, and seniors play such iconic roles as the King of Siam ("The King and I"), Dorothy ("The Wiz"), Danny Zuko ("Grease"), and Maria ("West Side Story"). Students who would have never tried out for anything in the past, now find themselves being character actors, siblings who saw their older brother or sister cast in "Beauty and the Beast" now find themselves part of a musical ensemble. Many of our shows sell out on a regular basis.

Even more surprising is the distance to which our theatre participants have traveled to showcase their talents. In the past four years, student actors and crew members have performed two musicals for the residents of Plains and Americus, Georgia, home to former President Jimmy Carter, and have made such an impression that we've been asked to come back for an encore production. In fact, the St. Genevieve family stretches for 3,000 miles across the country, with former Presidents, Oscar winners, religious leaders, and family and friends of the faculty, staff, and students from several different states, all coming together to celebrate a "grand slam" in our own rich and cultivated "field of dreams."

When I consider how far we've come, I realize how remarkable this journey has been. Years ago, I found myself with the responsibility of building a theater arts program from almost the ground up, and discovered that with the support of my peers, the helpfulness of parents and friends, and the passion of our creative team, "if you build it, they will come." Today at St. Genevieve High School, we continue to build it, and they continue to come.

President and Mrs. Carter and Shirley Jones with the St. Genevieve cast of "Carousel"

Athletics. St. Gen's currently has 31 teams, and more than 60 percent of our students participate in athletics at some point during the year. Over the years, I have seen the incredible influence a good coach can have on the academic and spiritual — as well as the athletic — formation of a youngster. Unfortunately, there are far too many self-serving and glory-seeking coaches who put their own needs above those of their athletes. It is imperative for schools to clearly identify the goals of their athletic programs and hire coaches who will adhere to those goals.

Who's Winning?

by Marlon Archey, Athletic Director, St. Genevieve High School

As most of us know, high school athletics have become a major attraction for improving enrollments around the country. I work every day to keep the St. Genevieve High School athletic program unique and fun for our students. Fun? Isn't it about winning? That's the question that we all face — from the highest divisions to the lowest — and sometimes, it's interpreted to mean winning at all costs. At St. Genevieve High School, we strive every day to be victorious by practicing our school's mission statement: "To Know God, To Live with Honor, To Change the World."

When I accepted the position of Athletic Director thirteen years ago, I inherited the longest losing streak in division 13 CIF football. Not only were we losing games on the field, we were also losing the respect of our community because the behavior of our coaches, players, and general school population was far from sportsmanlike. I faced the monumental task of overcoming low morale and a negative reputation for being "thugs." This proved to be my greatest hurdle. Our  students were embarrassed and ashamed to participate in sports, and most definitely were not interested in wearing athletic apparel that promoted the school. The mountain at times seemed very steep, but our implementation of a character education program was the foundation we needed to turn around a failing school and athletic program.

We saw character education as the answer to saving the school from closing and to promote an athletics program that featured good sportsmanship and integrity over the need to win at all costs. The Valiants decided to speak with "one voice" in the classrooms, hallways, athletic fields, and sports courts. Our mission was simple: to develop a school and an athletic program of honor and integrity. We knew that we had the power to change lives through athletic competition, and our first goal was to change the negative perception and reputation of St. Genevieve athletics.

First on the agenda was to hire new coaches. We knew we needed coaches who were educators and role models first, before just concentrating on x's and o's. We needed men and women who were willing to possibly sacrifice winning on the scoreboard in favor of becoming victorious in the modeling and shaping of our student-athletes.

Before the hiring process began, we enlisted parents, teachers, students, and established coaches to create questions that went beyond the scope of coaching, delving into the character and moral values of our candidates. I conducted the initial interview before passing a potential coach on to the next phase. Phase two was a panel of parents, teachers, school counselors, and student-athletes, all of whom asked relevant questions to further the evaluation process. Once a candidate moved on to phase three, he or she was asked to run a mock practice with the appropriate team. Phase four was a final interview with the school's administration.

Our hiring process has since become a model for many high schools throughout southern California. We believe that even though winning is typically the objective of a sport, when coaching the student-athlete, learning life lessons is what should be the main goal. This approach may not be popular with schools that believe in winning at all costs, but we've found that developing the whole person and leveraging a favorite sport as a tool for character formation and growth is what works best for our school.

With building integrity and character at the heart of our program, coaches here serve as motivators, role models, parental figures, and mentors. We have experienced great success with this approach as is evidenced by some of our recent statistics (compared to our stats prior to implementing our character education program):

- From 1990 to 1999 (before implementing our character education program), 11 different teams qualified for the CIF playoffs, while from 2000 to 2012 (after implementing character education), 97 different teams have qualified for the CIF playoffs.
- From 1990 to 1999 (prior to character education), less than 40% of students participated in sports, whereas in 2012, more than 60% of students participated in sports.
- From 2000 to 2012, St. Genevieve teams have won 14 league championships as compared to just 3 championships won between 1990 and 1999.

Our hope as a school is that our student-athletes will understand the true meaning of the "six pillars of character" by implementing them in their daily lives on the playing fields and courts. Our coaches are expected to promote good sportsmanship and fair competition among our own teams as well as those of our opponents. For example, whether we were on the winning or losing end of a football game this past season, our coaches and players invited the opposing team to pray with us, led by our head coach. As our coach explained, "This is a beautiful lesson — your opponent is not your enemy, he is your brother that you can lift up through Christ."

When I see moments like this transpire at the center of a football field, I know that we have reached the top of that mountain that seemed so steep thirteen years ago. To watch our girls' soccer teams experience success over the past ten years by winning eight league titles and finishing the last four years undefeated in league play is a major triumph. However, it has been even more rewarding to watch those young ladies perform community service for churches, homeless shelters, and other organizations serving underprivileged youth. The combination of winning on the field and within the community is what describes a "true champion."

Over the past year, there have been times that I have sat at my desk and marveled at the accomplishments of our school, and specifically, the successes that we have experienced athletically. I am amazed yet overjoyed by the many enthusiastic emails from parents, complimenting our coaches about how they have influenced the lives of their children. I am incredibly gratified by the numerous phone calls I've received from opposing schools and spectators who have been impressed by the conduct of our players and fans.

I can think back thirteen years ago to when our athletic department was in shambles and this was the last place that a coach wanted to coach or a student wanted to participate in athletics. In those days, it was quite common for a coach to miss practice — or even a game

— because the feeling was, we were going to lose anyway. Today, our school is filled with positive coaches who see teaching life lessons as their major objective, and who actually make winning fun. As our Principal, Dan Horn, explains in our athletic mission statement, "More than any title or award, we are most proud of the sportsmanship and determination that our teams consistently display. That is what will mold their futures."

St. Genevieve student-athletes understand that their objective is much more than winning a game on a Friday or Saturday night. Their true objective is "To Know God, To Live with Honor, To Change the World." That is victory at its best!

Campus Ministry. As our school has grown, so too has our campus ministry program. Considering that we don't have a full-time campus minister, what we accomplish is rather extraordinary. The credit is due to our amazing staff. To be a successful teacher or staff member here means being someone who sees him- or herself as a campus minister. Everyone gets involved in the spiritual development of our students and the spiritual life of our campus. The spiritual life for a staff member at St. Gen's is a rather intimate experience. We do our best to describe this to applicants up front. It takes someone who is securely on his or her own spiritual journey to be able to teach here. More and more students are also getting involved in campus ministry. A few years ago we decided to implement the Kairos program, which takes a huge commitment from students and staff, especially in a relatively small school. Most of our faculty members have been on a Kairos retreat — we do three a year — and those who stay behind substitute for the four days of the retreat for those staff members who are away.

Ensuring the Success of Kairos

by Dennis Yumul, Campus Minister, St. Genevieve High School

Kairos 23. Another successful retreat. As the ceremony ends, I look around the gym and see many happy faces. There are parents and their children hugging and kissing. Fathers are trying to hold back the tears of joy as they hug their sons. Mothers are holding onto their daughters' hands, not wanting to let go. It is moments like this that make it so fulfilling to be a part of the campus ministry program at St. Genevieve High School.

As the families walk out of the gym, I get a number of "thank you's," some pats on the back, and quite a few hugs, all for having led the school retreat. While I humbly accept the praise, I can't help but feel that I should not be the only one receiving these thanks. I know that the ones who make moments like this possible often seem to be left unappreciated.

Here at St. Genevieve High School we pride ourselves on our dedication to the spiritual growth of our school. We believe that the catechesis we provide allows our students to achieve the mission of our school, which is, "To know God, To live with honor, To change the world." Through our religious studies classes, Masses, service hour program, and many other opportunities, students are able to develop a faith life that they can take with them once they graduate.

One of the opportunities we offer is our Kairos retreat program for seniors. Literally meaning "God's time," Kairos is an adolescent version of the Catholic Church's Cursillo program that the Jesuit order developed especially for high school students. It is meant to allow students to take time out to develop a deeper bond with themselves, their classmates, and ultimately, God. The Kairos program is offered in schools throughout the country, with each school bringing its own inspiration to the program. At St. Genevieve High School, Kairos has been uniquely crafted and fully embraced by everyone in the school, from teachers to students.

Students take a very active part in the program. During their freshmen and sophomore years they are introduced to the program and see the impact it has had on the lives of the seniors who have participated. Many seniors have told me that they knew ever since they were freshmen that they would be leaders at their Kairos retreat. During their junior year, students can take part in the Junior Kairos leadership retreat, which gives them the opportunity to be leaders during their senior year. Seniors become the leaders who organize and prepare the Kairos retreat, ensuring the success and continuation of the program. Beyond the retreat, they also become active members of the campus ministry leadership team throughout the year.

Of course students are not the only ones who make this program possible. St. Genevieve faculty and staff also are key to the program's success. As many as eight teachers take four days out of their busy schedules every few months, away from their family and friends, to go on a Kairos retreat. They lead the retreat along with the senior leaders, giving their time and sharing their experience. The teachers' personal interactions with the students have made a huge difference, as students get to see the love that their teachers have for them. Other staff members also join in the leadership; in fact, a majority of the St. Genevieve faculty and staff has taken part in the program.

In addition to the teachers who go on the retreat, there are still others behind the scenes who may be forgotten. For example, teachers who stay behind also contribute to the program. They have to substitute teach the classes for those who are away at Kairos. A number of teachers stay until 10:00 p.m. on a weeknight to prepare prayer services for the parents of the Kairos students. The athletic department works in conjunction with the campus minister to schedule the Kairos retreat. The athletic coaches and club moderators also work with the students and the campus minister to make sure that the students can be a part of the retreat. In other words, each member of our school participates in making our Kairos retreat program a success.

This cooperation and support can be found in every aspect of campus ministry. Whether it is our liturgies, our retreats, or our service hour program, the entire school participates and celebrates what we do. I believe that this is one of the many things that makes our school unique. We all believe in our mission. We all have the same purpose. And even though we may have different jobs and priorities, we know that at the end of the day we all have the same goal: to teach our students "To know God, To live with honor, To change the world."

Clubs and Other Activities. Depending on the year and the interest level of the staff, we offer a variety of clubs and other activities, ranging from an Animae Club to Mock Trial. The wise school administrator realizes that not all students are interested in athletics or the arts, and by providing an opportunity for students to meet on campus to pursue their diverse interests, offers a valuable resource for teaching teamwork and leadership skills.

Mock Trial: More Than Just Students

by Ryan Halverson, Government and Economics Teacher, St. Genevieve High School

As a first year teacher at St. Genevieve, I was very excited to get involved in new activities where I could mentor beyond the classroom. One of those opportunities came my way when sophomore English teacher, Mr. Norman, extended an invitation to assist him with reviving the Mock Trial program at our school. I'm not sure if he asked me to help because I exhibited the qualities he was looking for in a co-coordinator or simply because I was new and looked gullible. I like to believe it was the former.

I had absolutely no Mock Trial experience. Well, I knew what Mock Trial was, so I guess that had to count for something. But I had never coached it or participated in the program when I was in high school. I'm also less than confident that my semester of law school in 2003 could be used as any kind of foundation for understanding legal procedure. All that being said, I accepted the invitation with uncertain eagerness.

In the course of preparing a schedule and a process for how to promote and begin the after-school program, I came to realize that Mr. Norman also had no prior experience with Mock Trial, which actually made me feel strangely better about the endeavor. At least I would have someone to share in the confusion.

After announcements, sign-ups, and auditions, we started to get an idea of who our team would be. All but one of the students on our team, like their coaches, had no previous Mock Trial experience. What we lacked in experience, we made up for in teamwork and preparation. But we only had about two-and-a-half months to prepare for the competition.

Many St. Genevieve students are involved in multiple activities, and their different schedules put pressure on our team to get quality practices in during our after-school practices and lunch meetings. However, the students were willing to be flexible when we allowed them to be. And as the competition dates approached, the anticipation helped to bring us closer together as a team.

To be honest, I was not prepared for the magnitude of the competition. After a full day of work and an afternoon of Mock Trial practice, we loaded our team onto the school busses. Our lawyers, witnesses, bailiffs, and timekeepers were all in tow and dressed the part.

When we arrived downtown at the Los Angeles County Court House, the Mock Trial teams were entering as the real lawyers and court personnel were exiting. We located our assigned courtroom, and sat in the hallway for what seemed like an interminable waiting period. Some of the students sat quietly and alone, seeming to be running through everything they'd learned within the silence of their minds. Others paced, notes in hand, mumbling reminders to themselves, while lawyer and witness teams huddled in small groups, actively reviewing and working out kinks.

Once we entered the courtroom and the real judge began the competition, all Mr. Norman and I could do was sit quietly and watch. We were not allowed to have any interaction with our team. It felt like letting your toddler ride a bike without training wheels for the first time. You want to offer support, but you know that you have to let them take the ride on their own.

The whole experience felt like watching an intense

thriller. At some moments I was gripping the armrest of my seat, white-knuckled and teeth clenched, while in other moments I was biting my fist to stop from yelling out an excited "YES!" in the courtroom. But that's also what was so great about the experience. It was incredibly satisfying getting to see students be successful outside of the classroom, seeing them realize their true potential, and being able to know that you were part of this moment and part of the journey.

During our post-competition debriefing with the team, it was hard for me to restrain my complete and utter enthusiasm. I was on an emotional high and was definitely having fun. The bus ride home was equally as fun. Students were breaking down the event like a play-by-play announcer. They'd had fun, too. I think that learning while having fun is what it's all about. My number one goal as an educator is to instill a love of learning in my students, and here I was, seeing that goal being fulfilled. Moments like this may be attainable in different ways and in different places, but there is something truly special about spending time with a group of students outside of the general education classroom. You get to see them in a different light and they get to see themselves in a different light as well.

The Question of Stipends

In my years at St. Thomas, Colleen O'Shaughnessey and Joe Walsh, the volunteer dance teacher and the Broadway actor/ kindergarten teacher, never received any financial compensation for the years of incredible work they did in building a quality and lasting theater arts program for St. Thomas School. Similarly, when I arrived at St. Genevieve, the school's budget simply did not allow for stipends to be given to people for all the extra time they put into making a variety of significant contributions to our school's culture. However, as corny as it may sound, I have discovered that the gift of words can be of great value; I have discovered this value both in the giving and in the receiving.

Sincere Expressions of Gratitude. We've all been on the receiving end of platitudes. They seem so meaningless. However, when someone takes the time to write — or say in person — sincere words of gratitude, taking time to comment on things that many people barely notice, it can mean a great deal. In some cases, it can mean even more than money.

Small Tokens of Appreciation. Whenever possible, a small token of appreciation should be given for extra time put in or work done voluntarily. Even if it isn't always fully appreciated, it is the right thing to do. You are representing your school, either as pastor, principal, or classroom teacher. Whenever someone has done something for your community, why not help to create a culture of gratitude? So often we think nothing of asking, yet we think so little of offering gratitude. What great lessons for the students in our school to be taught to always be grateful — to pray for someone who has gifted us with their time, talent, or treasure, and then write a note to tell them we prayed for them. Why not do it even if it is for another teacher in the school or a parent within the community? I was truly touched when, after making a presentation for one of the financially challenged schools in our community, I was given a thank-you card containing an American Express Card that paid for a tank of gas for my car. That warmed my heart. On the other hand, I've sometimes been asked to give a presentation by schools or other groups with obvious financial means and have been given a handshake and a smile for my time, but had to pay for my own parking. The smile and handshake were nice enough, but in those circumstances, the lukewarm thank-you didn't make me feel super-appreciated.

An Actual Stipend. When possible, pay a stipend! I've heard Catholic school principals say things like, "Mrs. Soandso really doesn't need it, her husband has a good job." That's not the point. The point is, if you can afford to do it, then you should. As the financial gatekeeper for your school, you should. Let Mrs. Soandso give it back, or donate it somewhere else, but don't take it upon yourself to be judge and jury of someone else's financial affairs.

I have always found that when my schools have been able to afford to be fair and generous, people have tended to be fair and generous in return; it's the karma effect. Be caring, not judgmental. When you appreciate people, they tend to give back. When parents feel that their children are in an environment where they are cared for and have opportunities to succeed, they tend to stay.

Chapter 8: Themes to Live By

When I was an elementary school principal, I did not choose a theme for our school each year. In retrospect, I should have. It happened somewhat accidentally when I became principal of St. Genevieve High School, and I quickly realized I was on to something.

Although I did not officially begin my assignment as principal of St. Genevieve until July 1, 1999, I began thinking about the challenges that lay ahead as soon as I signed on the dotted line in April. "Demoralized" was the word that had been used again and again by most of the stakeholders who interviewed me when I'd asked them to describe the school's biggest challenges.

Devising a School Theme

Although I had faced many challenges during my years at St. Thomas elementary school, morale was never one of them. The morale there had been largely positive throughout most of my tenure. This would be a new challenge. And as I would soon discover, morale affects — directly or indirectly — every aspect of a school's culture and reality.

On April 20, 1999 I was on Easter break when the televised images of terrified high school students running from their suburban Colorado high school became burned into my memory. As the days passed, I, like so many Americans, waited anxiously for answers. The media quickly painted a picture of Dylan Klebold and Eric Harris as loners who had been bullied and teased by members of their school community and eventually were turned into suburban terrorists at the hands of their classmates. I was determined to somehow pay homage to the lives lost at Columbine by learning some lessons from it. I would use these lessons, I decided, to help build a new foundation at St. Genevieve High School.

Perhaps the biggest and most important lesson I learned came not from Columbine but from Chatfield High School. Two weeks after the tragedy, the Columbine students were sent to Chatfield High to complete the school year since Columbine would remain closed during the investigation. It would not open again until September.

I was as riveted watching the televised reports of the Columbine students walking into Chatfield as I'd been watching those same students running out of their own school two weeks earlier. They approached the new school with, understandably, looks of trepidation on their faces, but as the mass of students crossed the threshold into the building, their concerned-looking countenances dissolved into more relaxed expressions, with many students even breaking into smiles. Then the camera panned and showed me what they were seeing. Although the Chatfield students could not be there at the same time as the Columbine students — the building was too small to accommodate the populations of two schools simultaneously, so there would be split sessions — the Chatfield kids had plastered their walls and corridors with posters and banners of welcome; one the camera showed said, "We Love You!"

It was at this precise moment that I felt the inspiration I was looking for. This was the moment that my life changed and I knew St. Genevieve High School would be not only okay, but that we would eventually thrive. I knew right then what the first theme for the 1999-2000 school year at St. Gen's would be:

LESSONS LEARNED FROM COLUMBINE

I envisioned our school honoring the lives lost at Columbine by creating an environment in which:

1. All St. Genevieve students felt a sense of welcome and a sense of belonging. Everyone would have a place at the proverbial table of brotherhood and sisterhood that would become the new St. Gen's High School.

2. Teachers and students alike would be challenged to be at their spiritual best each and every day. We would be the school that would not wait for the disaster to strike to bring the best out in us. When one of us was not living up to our spiritual best, it would be the responsibility of those around us to remind us who God wants us to be. I was determined to become the Catholic school that could take down the name of the school and the crucifixes, and people would still know they were in a Catholic school by how they were treated.

The Importance of Being Important

by Amanda Allen, Development Director, St. Genevieve High School

It may sound rudimentary, but the fact is, we all want to feel important, and we all want to feel as if our presence makes a difference to those around us. St. Genevieve High School is good at making its students feel important, plain and simple. Also plain and simple: when we make our students feel important, our ability to retain them through graduation significantly improves.

Although I have only been at St. Genevieve High School for six months, I've had a palpable sense from my very first day, of students, teachers, and administrators all working toward a common goal. You can feel it in the classrooms and the hallways, in the library and the gym. It's the culture here. Unified through our mission statement — "To know God, To live with honor, To change the world" — each stakeholder has an acute awareness of the critical role he or she plays in the sustainability and long-term success of the school.

One of the most basic and simple tasks St. Genevieve students are charged with is to greet adults with a handshake. It is a powerful thing to see young men and women walking down the hall stop to shake the hands of the principal, prospective parents, teachers, alumni, and other visitors, with a "good morning" and a "thank you for visiting our school." Students understand what an important role this is and how they are the only ones who can have the impact they do on visitors to the school.

Giving students an authentic purpose and a way to

fulfill this purpose — like shaking hands and greeting visitors — makes them feel as if they are needed (which, of course, they are), and as if their presence makes a genuine difference at the school (which, of course, it does). Thanking them for their help further reinforces that we need them just as much as they need us. These interactions create a mutual respect and partnership between the faculty/staff and the students.

When students (and faculty!) feel valued and needed, their commitment to their school is enhanced, as is the likelihood that they will continue on with the school. Such is the case at St. Genevieve High School.

The Value of Themes

Although it was my tenth year as a principal, in that first year at St. Gen's I discovered something. I learned that having a school theme acted as a kind of guiding force, a reminder throughout the year that we were there for more than just academics.

For my second year at St. Genevieve, it seemed only natural that our theme became LESSONS LEARNED FROM ST. GENEVIEVE.

What were the lessons we'd learned that first year together as our school's morale began to shift? When we had started talking about Columbine High School rather than studying from a textbook that first year, one of the first things our students told us — loudly and clearly — that very first week was, "We want more days like this!" They liked taking a break from their texts and talking about subjects that mattered to them. Thus, our character education program was born.

So, guided by our second-year theme of LESSONS LEARNED FROM ST. GENEVIEVE, we attempted to formalize and strengthen what eventually became our character education program.

When there were issues of cheating, we developed a lesson plan using the HBO movie "Cheaters," dividing students into "family" homerooms, where some fairly intense discussions about cheating took place. It was interesting (horrifying?) to discover how many students these days believe there's not much wrong with cheating as long as you don't get caught. I suppose it's not hard to imagine why this is when we live in a society where kids see adults regularly making decisions to cheat — from banks providing unrealistic mortgages and loans to people who will not be able to honor their obligations, to teachers who change answers on standardized tests in order to keep their jobs or perhaps secure a bonus from their district.

As an elementary school principal, I often had to deal with the sad irony of parents lying right in front of their children. A common scenario was one in which a parent brought their kindergartner or first-grader to school late and I'd ask the student, "Why are you late?" The parent would typically let fly an obvious lie like "the car wouldn't start" or "we got a flat tire," only to having a smiling (and honest) son or daughter provide the real truth: "my mommy didn't get up on time" or "we stopped at Burger King." My eyes would go directly toward those of the lying parent, who often tried to avert my gaze. At that point, I would say to the child, "Thank you for being so honest with me this morning!"

So, if the schools don't take the time to teach character and instill values, I'm not sure it will get done at all. Those of us who teach in Catholic schools — especially those of us who are on the edge of closing our doors — have a real opportunity to develop cutting-edge curriculum that is truly crucial to the success of our nation. Don't think that teaching character is being done in the religion classroom down the hall — it is the responsibility of each and every one of us.

When you're entering into a relationship of any kind — romantic, business, or even simply with a new neighbor — does it really matter where that person graduated from if he isn't ethical and honest? Does it really matter what someone's SAT scores were if she doesn't respect you, your family, or our nation?

It's interesting how classroom conversations about cheating can get turned around very quickly when students are engaged by questions such as: would it be okay if the doctor about to perform brain surgery on your mother had cheated during medical school? Would it be okay if the pilot about to fly you overseas had lied or cheated to get into that cockpit?

It's not really our jobs to tell students what or how to think, but I do believe that our job as educators in today's world is to provide students with opportunities to clarify their values. And it helps to do so by providing cutting-edge and meaningful curriculum, which I've found develops far more easily and organically when you're guided by a strong theme.

I Love My Life

For the 2012-2013 school year, our school theme is I LOVE MY LIFE. One of the main reasons for this beautiful theme is simply the fact that it *is* a beautiful theme, and my guess is that most of our teens have seldom, if ever, said these words until this year.

I believe that to be successful in teaching children, especially teens, we have to teach them to affirm themselves. After all, who else is doing it? Parents are often too busy. Lets face it, we typically teach the way we've been taught, and we parent the way we were parented. Many parents simply don't affirm their children because they were never affirmed themselves. Many teachers don't affirm their students for the same reason. We are so quick to point out the negative because that's the experience we had as students ourselves.

As a new teacher and then again as a new principal, I was also leery of being seen as too much of a Pollyanna type. My fear was that if I were too complimentary, people would not take me seriously. Boy, was I ever wrong. By the time I got to St. Gen's, I fortunately had learned the power of positive reinforcement. It changed all of our lives.

Don't get me wrong. I'm not saying that people should not be corrected when they make mistakes. But I've learned that the vast majority of people like to please others and be recognized for it. So, if you as a teacher or principal spend most of your time pointing out people's accomplishments (instead of mistakes), it will cause others to try to make positive contributions as well. In my early years at St. Gen's, it was tough to find the positive things that were happening on our campus. Now, an overwhelmingly positive energy abounds! It has been a truly stunning turnaround.

You cannot imagine the pleasure involved in being the chief affirmer. When people hear what I do for a living, I usually receive the standard, "Gee, that must be a tough job." My standard response is, "Most days I love it."

Who wouldn't love a job that provides such a tremendous source of positive energy? So often I say to people, "You have to come onto the campus to believe the energy here. You must experience it yourself." However, I never take our school's energy for granted, and I continually work to make it consistent, to make it better when it begins to ebb, as it inevitably does. I constantly remind teachers that our environment is something we must all contribute to and work at every day.

To align with our 2012-2013 year theme, we rewrote the lyrics to the Four Seasons' "Opus 17 (Don't You Worry 'Bout Me)," so that by the end of the song, the students have sung the words, "I love my life" at least six times. We sing it at all of our special events and at most of our Masses throughout the year. The students love the Motown beat and the staff loves hearing hundreds of teenagers loudly singing those beautiful and powerful words — it's all about affirming ourselves. I've included our rewritten lyrics for your enjoyment. After all, our words often become our reality.

I Love My Life So!

I can see
A new reality
A world created and inspired just for me
I used to feel so low
I didn't want to grow
There wasn't much to know
But now I LOVE my life so

I was blue
And I was cryin' too
But then the Lord transformed me into someone new
I learned my Savior died
It left my heart untied
I gave up all my pride
And now I LOVE my life so

I'll be strong
I'll sing my Savior's song
The love and strength He gave I'll always carry on
My life's no longer blue
I finally found the clue
My world's begun anew
Cause now I LOVE my life so
OOOOOOOOOOOOOO Aaa-Menn

I was shy!
To that I said good-bye
'Cause that's the part of me I'm leavin' high and dry
I'm not alone in pain
I'll never be ashamed
And you can feel the same
You gotta love LOVE your life so!

God loves you
No matter what you do
So spend your whole life living like He wants you to.
You gotta plant a seed
The hungry you should feed
And help the one's in need
And then you'll LOVE your life so.

I'll be strong
I'll sing my Savior's song
The love and strength He gave I'll always carry on
My life's no longer blue
I finally found the clue
My world's begun anew
And now I LOVE my life so.

Loving life with family members from Columbine, Beth Nimmo and son Craig Scott, center

In January of 2013 we hosted Beth Nimmo and Craig Scott as our guest speakers. Beth is the mother and Craig is the brother of Rachel Scott, the first student murdered at Columbine. Beth had visited us twice before, but this was Craig's first visit. As they remarked about the incomparable spirit of our school, I proudly told them how it all began with our first theme, "Lessons Learned From Columbine." At the evening's conclusion, our friends from Littleton, Colorado, caught up in the tremendous St. Genevieve spirit, joined our students in singing this year's theme song, "I Love My Life So!" We were 13 years away from "Lessons Learned From Columbine," reaping the rewards of those harsh lessons. We had come full circle.

Chapter 9: Customer Service

I mentioned earlier that "Raving Fans," by Ken Blanchard was a book that made a major impact on our lives here at St. Gen's. I recommended that the entire staff read it together, as I felt it would make for great conversation and goal setting. Ken Blanchard basically makes the case that in our country we have grown accustomed to waiting in long lines for cold food and generally poor customer service so that when we actually receive good customer service, we often end up raving about the experience. The same can be true in many schools. So the business, or school in our cases, that offers a premium customer service experience is the school that creates raving fans — and thereby builds its clientele.

After we read the book, I presented our staff with two salary scales for the coming year. One included a nominal raise. The other included a $4,000 raise for every member of the faculty. My plan was this. If we set the right goals for the year and achieved them, we would create enough buzz in our community, and enough raving fans, that our enrollment would undoubtedly be affected. Positively. I had done my math and had come up with the number of incoming registered freshmen we would need by March 15th — freshmen registration date — to enable the $4,000 raises to be realized for the following school year.

Boy, did that make for an exciting faculty discussion.

You Don't Have to Reach for the Stars

I tried to simplify it for everyone. Don't reach for the stars.

Just think of the things that we are already doing that we could be doing better. Or, think of the things that we aren't doing but could be — and how we could do them better than anyone else.

Here (and also below) are a few of the things we decided on. We made agreements to return parent phone calls within 24 hours or sooner. We decided that when we had visitors in the building, we would all make an effort to greet them and see if they needed help. And if a visitor asked for a particular office or person, rather than just give directions, we would actually take the visitor there if we had the time to do so. And, we would encourage our students to do the same things we were doing.

Powers of Ten

Once a month, on a Friday afternoon, we provided faculty-meeting time for teachers to make positive phone calls to at least ten parents. No negative phone calls or bad news on Powers of Ten days. It had an immediate and tremendously uplifting effect. Talk about changing a paradigm! Parents are not accustomed to receiving positive phone calls and the reactions are always wonderful. I highly recommend doing this.

Positive phone calls can change a paradigm

Parent-Teacher-Student Conferences

We agreed to have all of a student's teachers present when a parent comes in for a conference. The student needs to be present as well. Too often, parents — and students — are called in to only hear the negative. We thought it was important for all involved, including all the student's teachers, to hear about good — as well as negative — things that are happening in different classes so that everyone gets as full and balanced a perspective as possible.

A Comfortable Place to Wait

We placed comfortable furniture in the reception area where parents and visitors wait. We also bought a flat-screen television, which at the time made us look rather futuristic, though not so much anymore, and we keep it tuned to CNN. Guests are always offered a bottle of water or a cup of coffee or tea while they're waiting.

Make yourself comfortable

The response to these efforts has been simply amazing. I regularly receive phone calls, emails, and letters from people struck — and touched — by the extraordinary welcome they receive at St. Genevieve High School.

Although we did not hit our targeted enrollment number that year, we did the following year, and I kept my promise of the salary increase.

Some other ideas you may want to consider to improve your current customer service:

Reception. Who answers your phone? This is such an important role that it's critical to have the right person in the right place for this one (as it is for pretty much everything). Too often I have called other schools and been "greeted" by an apathetic-sounding student — or even worse, an apathetic-sounding or downright rude adult — on the other end. There is no excuse for a rude or cold receptionist — get these people off the phones immediately! Either they change or they can't work there. It doesn't matter how long they have worked for you or how many children they have sent through your school — they are hurting your school. Give them instructions on how to treat people properly, and demand that they do it. If they can't, someone else can.

Call and Visit Your Own School. Walk into your own school. Is there someone there to greet you? Someone friendly and helpful? I walk through the front door at St. Gen's on a regular basis. I also call the school on a regular basis. It drives me crazy when our hold music is not playing...or when it's playing too long without a friendly human getting back on the line. I monitor these things because the little things add up.

Marquee. Does your school have a marquee? Who decides what is displayed? Is it monitored? Who is your audience? If you are under-enrolled, you should be using your marquee to entice new families, not to inform those who are already there. When I read our marquee, I look at it as though I am the father of a child currently in middle school. Does the information displayed appeal to me? Use the marquee to brag about your school! Tell all the passersby about your accomplishments, not that there is an early dismissal on Friday.

Website. Who monitors the school's website? Who is it designed for? Current parents? Prospective parents? Students? All of the above? Is it kept up-to-date? What kind of an image does it project? Discuss your school's website at a faculty meeting. What impression does it give? Is it effective, or more of an after-thought? These days most people are using technology to research places of business, and that includes our schools. If we're not paying attention to maintaining our website, we're likely damaging our own cause. Don't believe me? Check out the website of your nearest charter school and compare its website to yours.

Security. If you have security officials at your school do they know they are part of a customer service team? What type of attitude do they project? What do people tell you about your security staff? Do you watch how they interact with students, parents, and visitors? I've been to campuses where I've been treated like a would-be terrorist. Is that the way you want visitors — potential parents — to be treated by your personnel?

Security *and* customer service!

Security vs. Convenience. Security is of utmost importance, no doubt. After the massacre at Sandy Hook Elementary School, we are all going to be on higher alert. However, our campuses should not become so much like fortresses that prospective families and other visitors find it too difficult to get inside. Parents may like the security of an outer fence, but if it's too hard to figure out how to get onto your campus, you may never meet many future parents.

Call To Arms. Calling all librarians, cafeteria workers, janitors, coaches, and other personnel. Does every member of your staff, paid or volunteer, know that they are part of a customer service team? If not, call a meeting tomorrow! Inform every person who works at your school in any capacity that in order for your school to thrive, you must ALL be at the top of your game when it comes to customer service. Otherwise, the free charter school down the street will be enrolling your students.

Library staff: on the customer service team!

Signage. Are there strategically positioned signs telling people where your school is located? Where the school's entrance is? How to find the main office? Sometimes we assume that people will automatically ask or somehow just figure out where they should go. Oh, and when's the last time that anyone painted or updated your signs?

Parking. What is it like for visitors to park on your campus? Do you have spots that are clearly marked for visitors? Are they near the school entrance or main office?

Directions. Are the directions to your school conveniently located on your school's website? Don't forget to include instructions about where to park and how to find the main office.

Bottom line: customer service should be a top priority to help ensure the current and future success of your school.

We're In It Together: It Takes a Team to Build Enrollment

by Juan L. Jasso, Admissions Director, St. Genevieve High School

In July 2001, I became the new Admissions Director at St. Genevieve High School. Having previously worked right next door, at St. Genevieve Elementary School, I knew I was going to face some major challenges due to the high school's poor reputation. But I was ready to take on the task at hand. St. Genevieve High School had a new principal and was experiencing a renaissance; I was ready to be part of the rebuilding and transformation.

Admissions directors typically spent their time visiting 8th grade classes, hosting Open Houses, collecting applications, and proctoring the High School Entrance

Exam — not doing a major amount of marketing and recruitment. We took for granted that students would keep walking in the door. But if we wanted St. Genevieve High School to survive, this was something we could no longer take for granted. We needed to take action.

We set long-term goals and made sure that everyone on staff was on board. I was the Admissions Director, but if we were going to succeed, we had to all do it together. We would create a culture, an atmosphere in which everyone would feel welcomed. This welcoming environment would become our key to success in recruitment and retention of students.

Since my position had never really existed before at St. Genevieve High School, there were no guidelines; I had a clean slate. I decided to take a grassroots approach to marketing and set out to build a professional relationship with each principal and eighth grade teacher in the surrounding elementary schools. But because St. Genevieve High School had such a bad reputation, no one would return my calls or my emails. I didn't let this deter me. I decided to personally visit each school and befriend the one person who could get me a meeting with the principal: the school secretary. My job was to be on a first-name basis with each school secretary. I accomplished this with gifts: orchids, baked goods, t-shirts; I wanted our partner schools to know that I was the face of St. Genevieve High School and I was here to stay.

It took me a few months, but I was finally able to meet with each principal and 8th grade teacher. The primary goal of these visits was to personally introduce myself, but also to make it known that St. Genevieve High School was committed to making sure that each of their graduates continued their Catholic education regardless of finances. In turn, St. Genevieve made a commitment to providing financial assistance, whether we had a financial assistance fund or not! Filling an empty seat at a discount was better than having an empty seat. Also, colleges and universities charge international students a premium to attend their schools. If we did the same, that could help us provide financial assistance while also bringing a diversity of international cultures to our campus.

A school year came and went. We had a slight increase in our incoming 9th grade class. As we forged ahead, we encouraged our teachers to think outside the box to better engage student learning. We wanted to make sure that every student loved coming to school and loved learning. If we were going to compete academically with the better local schools, we needed to expand our offerings in Math, Science, Foreign Language, and electives. We were the first Catholic high school in Los Angeles to create a Mandarin language program. We brought back the Arts, Drama, Choir, Band, and Dance. But the most important subject we concentrated on was Character Education.

We knew that our support staff also would be key to the transformation of St. Genevieve, so we made a number of changes, including how we answered the phone. For example, the reply, "I don't know," was replaced by "I'll find out."

The school's physical plant was also a priority. If we were going to get potential parents and students to look at us, we needed to make sure we looked well maintained and, most importantly, clean. We remodeled our hallways, classrooms, library, and reception area. Once we were able to make a good impression, our first guests were my new friends: our partner school principals and eighth-grade teachers.

This was our opportunity to prove to our partner schools what St. Genevieve could offer to their graduates. We selected student ambassadors — preferably alumni from the visiting partner's school — as greeters and tour guides. The campus visit began with a campus tour, guided by student ambassadors. After the tour, we invited our guests into our Fellowship Center (aka faculty lounge!), where we were joined by our Academic and College Counselors, Athletic Director, Vice Principal and a few teachers for a working breakfast during which we had the opportunity to discuss our highlighted academic and extracurricular programs as well as our classroom curriculum and methodology.

The biggest change I made was my office hours. I no longer had the luxury of working from 7:30 a.m. until 3:30 p.m. We needed to show people the new St. Genevieve, and if that meant meeting a potential parent at 6:00 a.m. or 8:00 p.m., so be it.

We also tried new and creative ways to get people to our Open Houses. Having "evening days" of school during the week and hosting Saturday Open Houses for working parents proved successful. We eventually made Open House a regular day of school...on a Saturday! Yes, a regular day of school on a Saturday: we took attendance, teachers were teaching, students were learning. After all, how would our potential parents and students get to know us if they toured an empty campus? We began Open House with an informational assembly, which was more like a pep rally. With a gym full of St. Genevieve High School students, the energy is addictive. A recent phone message from a prospective parent described our Open House as "The half-time Super Bowl show of Open Houses." He also said he felt that his child absolutely had to attend St. Genevieve High School! His message is no longer an anomaly.

We sought to rebuild our school by transforming its environment. Our goal was not only to recruit but also to retain. We did it by working together to make sure that everyone here feels like the VIP they are. If your school does not have a vision and a mission that every single person on staff is able to believe in, there is no amount of cupcakes you can give your partner schools for them to believe in you.

Quick Reference Points:
- Grassroots marketing is key.
- Can prospective families find the entrance to your school?
- Cleanliness and a splash of paint can transform the campus.

- Customer service is everyone's responsibility.
- Are teachers available for students and parents or is there a race to the parking lot at 3:00 p.m?
- Make sure your partner school principals, eighth grade teachers, and school receptionist know you by name.
- Get partner school principals and eighth grade teachers on your school campus.
- Empty seats are lost revenue, filled seats at a discount equals additional money for operations.
- Get potential students on your campus. Provide incentives to schools to get their entire eighth grade class to visit your school for a Shadow Day. I provide permission slips, transportation, and lunch.
- Most importantly, what are your office hours?

Chapter 10: On the Road Again

When was the last time you or someone on your staff visited another school that you heard was doing great things?

I know, when we hear of good things happening at another school, it's easy to become jealous, especially when our own resources may be minimal. But jealousy is a waste of your time and energy. Envy keeps us small as individuals; it can overpower us on the job and keep our school small, too.

Envy is even worse when it takes place within the confines of our own school, especially when it leads to destructive behavior such as gossip among staff members. Few things can cause more to go wrong in a school than when teachers and staff are envious of one another and gossip prevails. If you tolerate gossip, I don't think you have the right to consider yourself a Catholic school.

What kind of conversations do staff members have about students and their families, or other staff members? A good rule of thumb: would you say what you're saying if the person you're talking about were standing right there? No? That's gossip! And to listen to gossip is to tolerate it.

What good does it do to leave a room, complaining, "I won't go into the faculty room anymore because the gossip gets to me"? You have just as much right to be in the staff lounge as anyone else, and you have a responsibility to say to those who are being negative or gossiping, "Let's change the subject."

When you hear of another teacher on your staff who is doing

an excellent job, you should feel proud that they are part of your team. You should want to learn from them and lift them up to the entire community. If, however, your first instinct is to feel jealous and say something negative, you need to look inward; you need to reflect upon your own personal growth rather than throw verbal stones in someone else's direction.

Learn From Others!

So when you hear about an exciting accomplishment at another school, you should run toward it. Make a point to go and see the program or the teacher first-hand. Find out how they do it, how they fund it.

When I was principal at St. Thomas school, each year every teacher and I would spend at least one full morning visiting another school we had heard good things about. Sometimes the school simply had more money and resources than we did, but we were able to adapt certain of their ideas to make them work for us.

Our staff at St. Gen's has now grown to a point where it is difficult to require every teacher to go out for a visit each year; however, we still make the effort. For instance, in the last few months we have sent groups of teachers to High Tech High School in San Diego as well as to a local charter school that has a blended learning curriculum, and to a local public school that offers innovative programs in peer counseling and conflict resolution.

It is always an honor to be asked by people if they can come to visit our school and see what makes us tick. Don't be afraid to ask your neighboring schools — and even those beyond — if you can visit. I'm sure that they'll be honored, too. And I'm sure that you'll learn something worthwhile.

Teacher Retreat

by Kara Ukolowicz, English Teacher, St. Genevieve High School

When you are a brand new English teacher looking for your first job and you find a clean and safe school with an opening, you will say yes to pretty much anything during the interview. I recall hearing of "retreat" for the first time during a brief introductory meeting with the dean of St. Genevieve High School, as I was being screened as a potential candidate. I was nervous, but I am sure she mentioned a week-long trip the staff takes in March as a contract requirement. Given my position (or lack thereof), I agreed, with little thought or concern about such a request. It seemed a bit strange, but, truthfully, the whole school did; there was music in the hallways and smiling kids around every corner.

I heard experienced teachers talk about "retreat" from time to time in the lounge or at meetings, but it never really entered into my consciousness as something to be either feared or anticipated. As a first-year teacher, I had plenty of other things to learn and worry about.

March seemed distant, and I really only began to think about it in the days leading up to departure. Even then, it was just a work commitment to be checked off the list of things to do before Spring Break.

I packed my bag, left my apartment and my dog behind, and arrived on campus around five in the morning to board a bus for Sedona, Arizona.

The shift begins immediately. With no papers to grade and no meetings to rush off to, people change. They reveal more of themselves. They let go and, fairly quickly, they begin to laugh.

We have had famous theological speakers as retreat guides. We have had difficult conversations about the mission of the school. We have sat in a circle and all talked about a loved one who passed away. We have had outdoor Masses set in nature's most holy landscapes. We've gone bowling.

Having now been on a number of retreats, I know that it is not what we do while we are gone that matters. What is important is that we take a week to commit to ourselves — and to one another — as a faculty and a family. Each year, the retreat activities differ, but the result is always the same. We become friends. I don't use this word lightly and I repeat, we are no longer merely co-workers; we are friends. It's easy to demonize the stranger down the hall, but when you have the opportunity to really get to know that person, things change. We know each other. We like each other. Friendship has the power to transform any faculty.

Having friends in every classroom on campus makes

me a better educator in ways that cannot be measured. Not only does it make us all willing to help one another, even more importantly, it makes us comfortable asking one another for help. So often, teachers become cloistered in their individual classrooms, fearing that asking for help is either a sign of weakness or ineptitude. This mentality keeps a school from growing. I have been asked to look at science lesson plans, review graded essays for fairness, and give a teacher a ride to school from an auto-repair shop. None of these strike me as unusual because I ask the same sorts of things of my friends all the time. At St. Genevieve High School, we work together as a cohesive unit. When a student needs a conference, we are all there, whether or not the student is struggling in our class. We are a team with a clear mission.

I look forward to retreat week now. In fact, it's my favorite week of the year aside from Christmas. I see it as time to spend catching up with friends. Teachers love to be busy; we are worker-bees by nature. It takes discipline to leave it all behind for a week, but I believe this "leaving behind" is critical to the success of the retreat. The retreat cannot be on campus and it cannot be just one day. Part of what brings us together is seeing the Dean of Discipline in his pajamas or realizing how hard it is for the teachers with children to leave their kids behind. It humanizes everyone on staff.

Back on campus, we have two separate lounges. One room is called The Faculty Fellowship Center and is used for daily meals and special events. It is a place to come together, but we are not allowed to work in this space. It is for communing only. The second lounge is a more traditional faculty room, with copiers, mailboxes, and computers. This is where we work during our break periods. It sounds nice, a separate space for work and for friendship. And while yes, we do not work in the one room, I challenge you to come on to our campus and find a single square inch in which fellowship does not happen every day.

Chapter 11: The Freshmen Retreat

Our school's Welcome Freshmen Day is always on a Friday. We schedule it for Friday because it takes a full week to prepare and the day itself is exhausting. The first Saturday after Welcome Freshmen Day is an overnight retreat for either the boys or the girls; we do them separately. The retreat is held at the school. This cuts down on costs because we don't have to rent a retreat facility. Plus, there is something symbolic about incoming freshman sleeping on the floor of our school's gym because our gym is like our family room; it is where we hold our Masses and other meaningful events. Our crest painted on the gym floor is like our family crest.

Senior students volunteer to lead the retreat, and together with our campus minister, plan appropriate talks and activities, including a midnight barbeque.

Welcome Freshmen Day activities

129

An Important Story

Each year I drop by both the boys' and the girls' retreats to pass on a story from the St. Genevieve High School Family History. On that night I always tell them the story of our once looked-down-upon school with its failing enrollment, bad reputation, and depressing reality. I then tell them how in the spring of 1999, the students at Chatfield High School welcomed the students from their rival high school into their own school with open hearts. They shared their classrooms, their lockers — their entire school — and did so with an overwhelming sense of welcome. On the first day, they had put up streamers and decorated their lockers and hallways with messages of hope and welcome. Because their school was not large enough to accommodate their rivals and themselves during the same hours, they did a split shift, and most of the Chatfield students never actually met the students from Columbine High School who needed a place to finish their school year.

I continue the story by telling the freshmen of the St. Genevieve students, who, during the 1999-2000 school year, had an opportunity to leave a legacy. They could have chosen to take the same path they had been on, which would most likely have resulted in yet another closure of a failed Catholic high school. Instead, they accepted the challenge to change directions because they knew in their hearts that they had an opportunity to begin to turn things around at St. Genevieve High School.

"Did you enjoy your first day as freshmen?" I always ask, to which I always get a resounding chorus of yeses. "Well you can thank the students at Chatfield High School, who inspired the St. Genevieve High School class of 2000 to choose to discover their best selves and leave a legacy of hope for the students who would follow them," I tell them. "You've been welcomed in a special way into a special place, and believe it or not, it is time for you as a class to begin to plan your own legacy. It is your job — your responsibility — now that you are here, to work to discover the best part of yourself as a human being, as a child of God. It is your job to treat every person you come into contact with at St. Genevieve High School with kindness, respect, and a welcoming spirit, as you yourself would like to be treated. We will encourage you to be at your spiritual best each and every day, and I expect that you will challenge your teachers — and me — to be good role models. I bid you good night ye new sons and daughters of St. Genevieve. Rest well, as you've got a big job ahead of you these next four years!"

A School Where Dreams Come True

by Regina Averion, Student, St. Genevieve High School

Every morning my day begins with zero period: Advanced Band. Since the 5th grade, I've always dreamt of being in a drumline, not only because of the challenge that comes with competing against other schools, but also because it involves being part of a team that shares a common goal. Now, as the current drumline captain of St. Genevieve High School, I am pleased to say that my dream has come true.

Although I was offered a spot in another high school's drumline, something about this high school really stood out: the Valiant community. There isn't a morning when at least one faculty/staff member, student, or a friend does not greet me. I always think to myself that these people *want* to be here. Sure, others can say that they feel very welcome within their group of friends, but at St. Genevieve High School, *the entire student body* is your group of friends. Everyone knows everyone here. The obvious bonds and support shared between everyone truly creates the community I'm fortunate to be a part of.

I practically live at school because I'm involved in so many activities. There's band, drumline, basketball, Associated Student Body, journalism, tech club, crew member on all of our musicals, and also Advanced Placement classes. Participating in each of these activities has given me memories that I would never have been able to experience at any other high school.

For example, as an aspiring musician, I was able to help the St. Genevieve drumline achieve first place at our first competition this past year. Other high schools have already participated in drumline competitions that stemmed from their past achievements, but this was St. Genevieve's first time, and we earned first place. The feeling of such accomplishment was something new because I helped make history in a way I've always hoped for.

Then there's my involvement with basketball at St. Gen's. Unfortunately, I tore my anterior cruciate ligament (ACL), which kept me from playing both my sophomore and my current junior year. Although I wasn't around much due to my recovery process, I will never forget that the team gave me a beautiful get well card just two days after my injury — which was so true to the spirit of the Valiant community. I've been injured in the past without anybody paying much notice, so this recognition from my teammates really made me feel like I'm at the place where I belong.

I also always work on the crew of the musical theater shows that St. Genevieve High School has become somewhat famous for. The fact that I was able to travel to Plains, Georgia with the cast and crew of our school's production of "Carousel" was phenomenal. We showcased our version of the musical at the Rylander Theater in Americus, Georgia for former president Jimmy Carter as well as for Academy Award-winner Shirley Jones, who played Julie Jordan in the original film. Throughout the week we were there, so many of the residents praised the St. Genevieve students for our positive and kind attitudes. President Carter also mentioned that his "favorite high school" happened to be St. Genevieve! Having a former president of the United States say that about the school you attend is not something you hear every day. In fact, it's something that students at any other high school won't possibly be able to hear! I was also able to learn about President Carter's early childhood years and experienced what's known as "Southern hospitality."

These are just some of the many reasons why I'm happy — and proud — to be a student at St. Genevieve High School. It's also the sense of family that I feel with the people at this school. It's the sense of constant strength given by the teachers, friends, and other students when I'm not at my highest. It's the fact that we remember what it takes to be a Valiant when another school insults us. It's the sense of teamwork I see throughout the days, whether through sports, music, or art. St. Genevieve High School is truly my home away from home, my second family, and the best alma mater I could possibly hope to have.

A High School Like No Other

by Vanessa Bass, Student, St. Genevieve High School

From the time I discovered St. Genevieve High School, I knew it would be the only high school for me. When I was first looking at high schools, I actually did not know much about St. Genevieve, but stepping onto the campus in the fall of 2008 for the Open House, I immediately felt the welcoming environment and saw teachers and students who truly and genuinely cared. Even though I was considering many other schools, I realized that I had found the right fit for me.

St. Genevieve is a place that welcomes everyone no matter who they are. There are no problems with bullying and nobody is afraid to be themselves. I have friends who transferred to St. Genevieve because they were unhappy at their high schools. One friend came as a sophomore because she was having a problem with bullying during her freshman year at another school. Once she came to St. Genevieve, she felt accepted and included in the warm school atmosphere here. She told me that she regretted even going to another high school, and never thought twice about her decision to transfer to St. Genevieve. The students at our school can interact with everyone because there are no cliques. Even the seniors talk and hang out with sophomores and freshmen because the culture of St. Genevieve is like one big family.

Teachers, staff, and parents also play an important role in creating an exciting and caring learning environment. The teachers truly care about the students and are always there for us. In class, the teachers design curriculum that is interactive, with class discussions and many group projects. After school, they are available for tutoring and are even available through email on the weekends. Our teachers always take the time out of their busy schedules to make sure that the students get the best possible support. Parents are also greatly involved and volunteer their time for booster club activities and other school events. When we have "evening days" of school, parents attend as well, which brings the entire St. Genevieve community together.

One of the many things that keeps me at St. Genevieve is the way our school involves everyone in school-wide activities, such as the annual trip to the Hollywood Bowl at the beginning of the school year. Our school is focused on the community and giving back, so in addition to our service hours, every Earth Day we go out and do something positive, such as picking up trash or removing graffiti from a park bench. We have also gone to a movie theater together as a school, for entertainment and educational purposes, to see "Avatar" and "The Help." The most recent movie we all saw together was a student-produced film about our school's trip to Georgia to perform the musical "Carousel" for former President Jimmy Carter and award-winning actress Shirley Jones.

At St. Genevieve, the opportunities are endless, and students are encouraged to get involved with many of the wonderful programs offered. During my freshman year I got involved in both the fall and spring musicals, and I also had the opportunity to go on a trip to China with some other St. Genevieve students. I have been dedicated to working on the school musicals ever since my freshman year, and I've played volleyball since my sophomore year. Along with these activities, I also have been involved in both honors and advanced placement courses, student government, and several other extracurricular activities. Now, as a senior, I've been given the opportunity to be a teacher's assistant for the dance class, so I help out the students in the class while also pursuing my passion for dance.

Looking back at my high school experience, I know that there is no other school out there that could live up to all that St. Genevieve has to offer. St. Genevieve is not a typical high school. When I come to campus, I know that I will get and give at least ten hugs every day. St. Genevieve is a school of character and this is demonstrated through the actions of all the teachers and students on campus. The overall school atmosphere is expressed through our mission statement: "To know God, To live with honor, To change the world." I am proud to call St. Genevieve my high school and I know I will always feel at home here.

Chapter 12: The Art of the Affirmation

St. Genevieve High School is an incredible place; there is no doubt about it. You only need to walk onto our campus and you instantly feel that something is special. How did we get this way? If you ask ten different people, you'll most likely get ten different responses. They would all be correct.

I am not certain which one thing works, or if you eliminated one or another strategy, if it all would still work. However, one thing of which I am certain: it began with a VISION…and a number of strategies to enable us to achieve that vision. One of those strategies is the art form of the affirmation.

Think about the happiest and most fulfilling moments of your life. My hunch is that they most likely were times when you experienced profound love and/or were being affirmed.

Look Your Kids in the Eyes

Author Toni Morrison once asked a group of parents, "When your kid walks in the room, do your eyes light up?" It's such an easy way to validate kids today when you're a teacher, yet we so often miss that opportunity. Just look at those kids when they're coming into the room. Look them in the eyes — for God's sake, for their sake, and for your sake. Have your lesson already prepared and stand at your door when they're walking in the corridors and coming into your room, and let them know you see them.

I will stand purposefully in our corridors or outside as the students are coming in, and I look them in the eyes to say, "Good morning," or, "Have a nice weekend." When students pass with their heads down, I take special note and make certain to greet them. If it's not too crowded, I try to shake as many hands as possible just to make that physical, human connection.

"Hey, come back here, now apply some pressure," I say if they give a weak handshake. "Great handshake this morning, thank you!"

Principal-student connections are so important

Look them in the eyes and greet them…by name preferably. With younger students in elementary school, this approach is rather easy. As they get to junior high and high school it becomes more challenging. Which only means they need it all the more.

It Doesn't Get Any Better Than This!

by Danielle Brown, Dance and Drama Teacher, St. Genevieve High School

When my husband was in his twenties, he used to take acting classes with a prestigious acting coach in Hollywood. When the scene work was stellar, the coach would say, "It doesn't get any better than this!" That phrase has stuck with me, and frankly, I have used it in my own teaching, because when you work with teenagers, and they "get it," you indeed see some of the best, most honest acting on the planet.

Teenagers do not necessarily have the emotional maturity to be supportive of their classmates. These kids are inexperienced actors, and I need to protect them from accidental slights. So I make it a point to indoctrinate them into the subtleties of scene-study decorum. They need to work toward becoming an ensemble because, as I tell them, "Some of you may get very emotional — some of you may even cry."

At the beginning of the year I don't think they really comprehend the validity of this statement, but as time unfolds they are initiated into the world of powerful emotions that can erupt from an actor delving into the raw and real emotion just beneath the surface.

A monologue is a speech given by a single actor. I ask my students to write their own so that they may achieve some reality when they perform. Sometimes the subject matter is "deep" and causes a visceral reaction in the student performer. Last semester, as one of my students proceeded into a section especially meaningful to her, grief began to bubble up to the surface. I stopped her and asked, "Are you okay to continue?" She said, "Yes."

When she then began to fully cry, I asked her to push through the tears and continue the monologue, but to restrain her tears. A scene is so much more powerful when the actor is fighting back the tears rather than giving in to the emotion. She held back her tears, but as they escaped around the barricades she erected, the scene became truly mesmerizing and touching. When she was done, the other students, who had been sitting in front of me watching her, whipped their heads around to me in disbelief and awe. They knew they had just experienced something very special that few people get to witness — the honest expression of emotion and the giving of one's trust to those you've only known for a short time.

I will never forget this experience, the expression on my students' faces and the performance of one young, raw actress, whose willingness to cry in front of her peers led to a deepening of an already growing bond between my students and me and between the students with one another. These kinds of bonds are so rarely achieved in a classroom, yet I find them consistently being formed at St. Genevieve High School, putting this school in a truly special class of its own.

Share Positive Feedback

Every time I get a positive letter about our school I read it to the entire school during our morning news broadcast. Each positive phone message gets played to the school, as well. We also often share the letters with parents at our evening events. At our most recent Open House, I shared a letter written by a 2012 graduate, which thanked our community for providing such a solid religious and spiritual foundation.

Each time someone shares a positive comment about our school or our students, I thank them and say, "I'll tell our students you said so." And I do my best to always pass on these positive comments to the student body during our announcements.

Morning Prayer Can Be Creative

I often volunteer to lead our morning prayer for the entire school. I try to be creative with prayer and, when possible, to always encourage students to find Christ within our school and within themselves. Some of my favorite times are leading students in positive and self-affirming school-wide meditations. Most recently, at twelve minutes past twelve on December 12, 2012, I interrupted classes to lead a gratitude meditation. "Here is a once-in-a-lifetime moment that we can all share," I said. "For the rest of your life, when you think about what you were doing on 12/12/12, you can remember this exact moment of 12 minutes past the hour of 12 and know that you and your entire school community joined together in thanking our Creator for the simple gifts of life — gifts like breath... hearing...sight...sound...smell...trees...friendship...and the ability to be grateful."

Showing Up

I know that the minute I walk into the gym, onto the field, into the play, or on the scene at any other venue or activity, that my presence gets noticed. I never take that for granted, however, and was taught long ago that there is a power to my presence. I do my solid best to make sure that all of our teachers and staff and as many parents as possible learn that same lesson. We've all heard the stories of the kid whose parents never show up. *I'm* there for that kid. I'm also there for the kids and the coaches who have all worked so hard to represent their school, and I encourage our teachers and staff to make every effort to be there as well. Obviously, I can't make it to every game, but I break my neck sometimes attempting to get to as many events as I can. I also encourage the coaches and players to not only notice but to say thank you to their parents, friends, classmates, and teachers who attend events — after all, affirmations work in both directions.

The Art of the Invitation

Tip O'Neil, former speaker of the U.S. House of Representatives, used to credit his winning elections every two years by never taking people's votes for granted. He never assumed that people knew he wanted their vote, he always remembered to ask them for it.

I often remind our students about that philosophy and over the years it has helped to transform our once almost empty bleachers and stands into the place to be for most events. Don't take it for granted that people know; there is power to the personal invitation. And when you take time to let people know you would like them to attend your event, that too can be affirming, if done sincerely.

Don't Neglect Your Faculty and Staff

Don't forget that your staff also needs and enjoys affirmations. There are times when I will devote an entire faculty meeting to matters of the spirit. Sometimes we will read and discuss a book together as a staff. Sometimes it's for the sake of business, like Ken Blanchard's "Raving Fans," which I've mentioned in other chapters, and sometimes it's for the sake of the spirit. A great read for a staff discussion is "The Four Agreements," by Don Miguel Ruiz. It's a short book that offers a great philosophy that we can all aspire to live by.

Committing to Partnerships

A few years ago, when morale at our school was getting better but was still far from great, and we all knew it, I devoted an entire morning to discussing the book, "Good to Great," by Jim Collins. We talked about issues we would like to address and set some goals for the year. The book had not been required reading, but it had certainly made a big enough impression on me that I made a presentation about it and led the discussion. To conclude the meeting, I called each person forward one at a time, looked him or her directly in the eye, and after saying the person's name, said, "I'm asking you to be my partner this year in transforming our school from a good one to a great one. Will you join me?" I had not planned to do this ahead of time, it just seemed like the right way to end the meeting. The room was dead silent. I waited for each person's response before calling the next person forward. It was my way of affirming my belief in each one of them, and I felt affirmed by each person's response.

Encouraging Student Leadership

I've already written about the importance of leadership among our senior students and all that we do to prepare seniors to help in leading the school. The final Mass of the school year is devoted to our juniors, as they're about to become seniors. Each of the juniors is called forward and I traditionally shake hands with each of them. I take the time to ask each of them to partner with me in the leadership for the coming year. I don't let go of a hand until the student looks me in the eye and provides a positive answer to my question. It is an affirming moment for both of us.

Sharing at the Staff Christmas Luncheon

As people were arriving at the restaurant for our most recent staff Christmas luncheon — 56 of us in all — I asked everyone to recall their favorite moment of the first semester. I gave them time to think of something rather than putting them on the spot; I tend to like to have time to think myself. Once we were all seated and being served, we went around the room and had each person share. It took almost 90 minutes, and I'm certain I speak for most if not all of us in saying that it was an incredibly affirming time. Together, our team had accomplished so many and such a variety of things in just that first semester that it brought both tears and laughter to all the tables.

Well Done!

First as a teacher and then as a principal, I realized that I was often hesitant to tell people that they'd done their work well. The fact is, most people have far more to compliment than to complain about. Therefore, I thought that if I was always complimenting people perhaps they would become lazy or not take my critiques seriously. I remembered my own English teachers, with their mostly negative critiques written in red ink, seeming as if they had bled all over my papers. I also remembered not paying much attention to all the negative comments and searching desperately for something positive.

It took a while for all this to sink in. When I became a teacher myself, I began correcting assignments in a variety of colors and always attempted to offer more positive than negative comments. I began to realize that if my students saw that I recognized their hard work and effort, then when I did have valid negative critiques, they would listen more carefully because they knew I wasn't only looking for flaws.

When I became principal at age 29, I had to re-learn this philosophy all over again. It somehow seemed preposterous for me to say to a teacher, especially one who was older than I was, "Well done!" or "I'm proud of you." Wouldn't they just laugh at hearing such things coming from me? Thankfully, it didn't take me too long to realize that I was operating from my own antiquated set of rules. I was denying my staff what they needed — and deserved — to hear largely due to my own insecurities.

My father died when I was only six. My mother, unfortunately, lived in large part by the "what will the neighbors think" mentality she had inherited from her mother. Therefore, compliments or encouragement were not in abundance in our house as I was growing up. As an adult in my late 20's and early 30's, I used to wonder, "Would my mother be proud of this accomplishment?" or, "I wish my father were here to see this."

Then, one glorious day, the truth came crashing down on me. It wasn't my parents' approval that I needed. It was my own. I realized that as long as I was proud of my own accomplishments, as long as I was proud of the man I had become — and was still becoming — I could then take that pride in myself and transfer it to others. I had become secure in who I was and quite happy with my own life.

I began to say to students and teachers, "I'm proud of you!" And I noticed that once I began saying this to students and staff members, I began to hear them saying it to each other. That, in itself, was something to be proud of. It is such an easy gift to give, why not give it every day?

Actually, I'm pretty proud of this chapter — now go and tell somebody that you're proud of them!

Did you do it? Well done!

Chapter 13: We Bow Before Thee

In November 2012 our school volunteered to be among the first to engage with a new accreditation protocol designed by the Western Catholic Education Association (WCEA), which, eventually, all Catholic schools will be using. Prior to this, we used Focus On Learning, an instrument provided by the Western Association of Schools and Colleges (WASC). The WCEA decided to have its own protocol, now titled Ensuring Educational Excellence, or E3. One of the main differences between the two accrediting instruments is that E3 has an entire section on Catholic Identity.

On the last day of our E3 accreditation visit, the five visitors and our entire faculty and staff held a meeting for final remarks. When it came time for the visitors to talk about our Catholic Identity, there was a pause, and the woman who was the chairperson of that section smiled and said, "When it comes to Catholic Identity, we bow before thee," at which point the room broke out into spontaneous and joyful applause.

That was a highlight, not only of the WCEA visit, but of my entire principalship at St. Genevieve High School. It was, to say the least, affirming.

Chances, Possibilities, and an Unintentional Math Teacher

by Tim Anderson, Math Teacher, St. Genevieve High School

Fresh out of college in 2004, I was tipped off to a job opening as an assistant in the counseling office at St. Genevieve High School. My duties were to manage the alumni database, pull transcripts, and perform a variety of other office tasks. I would show up at 7:30 and leave at 3:30. I am a musician, and this job was exactly what I was looking for. Spend my mornings making money and my evenings making music in my studio space in downtown Los Angeles.

Allan Shatkin, St. Gen's college counselor and music director, soon found out about my musical ambitions and gave me the task of spending some recently acquired grant money on a brand new PA system. A couple of thousand dollars later, our school had a rock concert-quality amplification system for our Masses, and I had a new addendum to my job description: sound engineer. This was mutually beneficial for the school and me. St.

Gen's is very well known for our larger-than-life Masses and professional-quality musicals, and I take a lot of pride in being a part of that. My first year at the school was a success, and I was feeling less and less temporary as each day went by, especially when things changed drastically the next fall.

Our geometry teacher had a baby at the end of the summer and was going on maternity leave for the first two months of the semester. The football coach at the time was going to fill in until her return. He only lasted two weeks. I got a call telling me to drop my office duties because I'd be substitute teaching all day. That day turned into two days. Then three. Then the rest of the week. There was talk of hiring another substitute or trying to get the previous geometry teacher to come back early, but in the meantime, I was just hanging on day by day. I was teaching, creating homework and quizzes, and even purchased a grade book. I never would have imagined myself doing this, but I was having a blast.

Meanwhile, while maintaining my office duties, I was also in charge of finding my math class replacement. During my lunch breaks, I was placing ads in the *Los Angeles Times* and on Monster.com. It was a surreal experience watching candidates come in to teach a mock lesson to "my class." Fortunately for me, there must have been a bad crop of math teachers around in late 2005 because I was asked to finish out the semester in the classroom. The previous geometry teacher was not going to return from maternity leave and the school was looking into hiring a full-time math teacher for the spring semester.

But clearly, I wanted to be in the classroom. So, I gained the courage to ask Dan, our principal, if I could finish out the school year teaching geometry. He took a chance on me and granted my wish. I joke with our teachers that I'm now in my eighth year of substituting, but these eight years have truly been amazing.

Working on our school's musicals, for example, has taken me across the country to Georgia twice to perform for President Jimmy Carter. I've led a group of our African-American students to Atlanta to tour the city's historically black colleges. I've led a retreat to Mexico and celebrated morning prayer with the Pope at the Vatican. I've spent many afternoons at the park coaching our softball team, and knocked down a few pins as the bowling club moderator. I've also spent many nights in another classroom downtown where I'm about to complete my master's and credentialing program.

I've had many adventures since joining St. Genevieve, and recently finished one of the greatest: leading the school through its accreditation process. I was very flattered when Dan asked me to help lead this important process. It showed me how far I'd come in what feels like a short time. It showed me that I'd become so ingrained in the culture of the school that I'd become one of its trusted "experts," entrusted to lead our faculty in more than a year-long self-study. In the end, we received the highest accreditation available to our school, with six years until the next visit. And it all goes back to Dan taking a chance on me in 2005, and giving me the opportunity to prove my potential.

There's actually something important to be said about this opportunity that I was given. That this opportunity existed for me and I was able to succeed is, I believe, a testament to Catholic schools. I was being completely honest when I said earlier that St. Genevieve and I were mutually beneficial for one another. Our stories are very similar. When I first started here, we were both turning over a new page in our lives. All we had was our potential. My being able to grow along with the school has created a bond between us that has made my years here more than just a job. I take pride in what I've done, and I believe that my school takes pride in me. This is something that just doesn't happen often in public schools. They don't take chances. And if you don't take chances, you won't make real progress. I'll be forever grateful for the chance St. Genevieve High School took on me, and for the real progress we've both made — and continue to make — together.

Can You Be Nontraditional and Also Successful?

You might say that our approach to being a Catholic school is at times nontraditional. I'm simply building on the nontraditional — but highly successful — approach I took as principal at St. Thomas the Apostle elementary school. It was only after I had signed my first contract as principal of St. Thomas school that I took the time to read the job description. When I came to the line that read, in part, "the principal is the religious and spiritual leader of the school," I choked on the Mountain Dew I was drinking. I began to worry and wonder about what I had gotten myself into — and what I had gotten that school into. I was to become the first lay principal in the school's more than 80-year history. Prior to me, all the principals had been nuns.

I could not easily quote scripture. I was lousy at leading impromptu prayer. I was not someone who regularly read his

Bible. I quickly began to think that I was the wrong man for this position. Then, I began to reflect on my twelve years spent in Catholic schools and of my early life, so much of which had been spent playing in and around our Catholic parish, Sacred Heart, in Jeannette, Pennsylvania.

Many of us who attended Catholic schools in the 60's and 70's have plenty of stories about some bitter and cruel nuns and priests. They could sure quote scripture and spout dogma, but when it came to actually walking the talk, they too often became sidetracked. How could Sister Soandso be talking one minute about Jesus and how much he loves each and every one of us, and the next minute be smacking Barry Benson with a ruler? Didn't Jesus love Barry? Sister certainly didn't seem to care for him too much.

Of course I'm not saying that all the nuns and priests treated us poorly. In fact, it was because of my second-grade teacher, Sister Juliana — who was so kind to each of us and inspired me to set up a classroom in my basement at home — that I first began to think of myself as a teacher. And then, of course, there were plenty of lay teachers who were quite mean and cruel as well.

But one thing I learned for sure during my twelve years of Catholic schooling is that just because one takes vows and wears a collar or veil, does not automatically make that person more qualified than anyone else to lead a Catholic school. Another thing I felt quite confident about after my years in Catholic schools was that I did know Jesus the Christ.

So after a couple of days of reflection about whether or not I could actually lead St. Thomas the Apostle School, I looked at that job description with an entirely different set of eyes. I was now confident that not only could I lead the school both religiously and spiritually, but that I would do an excellent job.

I would lead based upon my personal relationship with God and my belief in the goodness and kindness of his son, Jesus. And that's exactly what transpired, as I led St. Thomas school for nine perhaps nontraditional, but nevertheless successful, award-winning years.

What Makes a Catholic School?

Now, as principal of St. Genevieve High School, I've heard some more traditional Catholics make comments such as, "That school's not Catholic enough." Someone, allegedly a former student, even wrote an anonymous comment on one of those online school review sites that the school was "corrupt with Dan Horn as the principal" because we held our school Masses in the gym! Corrupt? Really?

We are a Catholic school. We are a proudly Catholic school. To me, being Catholic begins with who we are and, even more important, who we are aspiring to become.

If your students go to Mass everyday, does that make you a Catholic school? What about if they go once a week? Once a month?

We don't have regularly scheduled Masses at St. Genevieve High School. However, when we do celebrate Mass, it is an event. In fact, I would be so bold as to say that Mass is now an event that the majority of our students and staff genuinely look forward to.

Most students now look forward to Mass

I vividly remember attending the first school-wide Mass with the St. Genevieve student body in the fall of 1999. It reminded me of the hundreds of Masses I attended as a child with my family and throughout my elementary school years. It was boring. We were in St. Genevieve Church, which is built for 1,300 people and there were only slightly over 300 of us in attendance. The organ played traditional Catholic hymns and only a few people joined in to sing. Even if the kids had been singing, it would have been difficult to fill the large church with our sound. Mercifully, the priest raced through the Mass, giving a homily in record speed.

There were plenty of issues to deal with my first year at St. Gen's, and Mass was not one I was quite ready to tackle. But I was developing a vision. Until then, I had attended Masses at two very joy-filled Catholic parishes in Los Angeles, St. Monica and St. Agatha. The only other times I'd enjoyed attending Mass was back in high school, at Greensburg Central Catholic, where Mass was held in the gym; it actually was an event I looked forward to as a teen. That gave me an idea.

Involvement Is Key

During my second year at St. Gen's, I moved Mass to our gym. I knew a number of priests who genuinely enjoyed being around young people and I began inviting them to our St. Genevieve Masses. We hired professional musicians and began including music that appealed to our kids.

I knew from my years in the classroom that the best way to make learning enjoyable and meaningful for kids is to get them actively involved. So I applied this same strategy to Mass.

Liturgical dancers at St. Genevieve H.S.

We asked the kids to do the traditional readings of the day as well as the prayers of the faithful. We also began to include students in reenacting the gospel and had them involved with liturgical dance. However, nothing we did had as much of an impact as holding music practices for the entire school before each Mass and event.

I requested that time be built into the schedule for students to report to the gym to practice the music we were going to sing for an upcoming Mass or event. At first, as any junior high or high school teacher can imagine, this was like pulling teeth; most students resisted. However, I was certain that it was their role at that point in time to act as though what we were asking them to do was totally uncool and a complete waste of time. I was also certain that it was our role to create an environment that would allow them to be themselves and admit that they, although teenagers, still liked to sing.

It didn't happen overnight. It took time and required holding tight to the vision. I knew these kids had it in them. Our school was fortunate enough to have found Allan Shatkin, a master musician (who was also a college counselor), to hire for one event, our Welcome Freshmen Day in 2000. I had asked the seniors on the football team to do a dance routine for the freshmen. Yes, they thought I was nuts, but I'd talked them into it. They ended up loving it and their dance routine got written about in the *Los Angeles Times*! (Now, by the way, the seniors on the team usually come looking for me to ask when they're going to start dance rehearsals for Welcome Freshmen Day.) Anyway, Allan was hired to play the piano and teach the boys to sing "Sugar Pie, Honey Bunch." He ended up having such a positive experience that he applied for a position and became the college counselor at St. Gen's and has been with us ever since.

Thanks to Allan's musicianship and teaching style, our kids eventually came around. A few years later, the culture had changed. No more pulling teeth at Mass practices. Now, having teenagers singing at Mass and at events is simply what we do here — it's who we are.

Each year Allan also works with me on rewriting a pop song to fit our school's theme so that it can be sung during Mass. Part of the secret to our success is to include self-affirming phrases in the new lyrics.

In the fall of 2008, when we unveiled an incredibly beautiful icon of St. Genevieve that had been painted by artist Howard Anderson and donated to the school by the artist and his wife Kathy, Allan wrote a beautiful song called "I Do Believe...St. Genevieve," and we have been singing it at various events ever since.

St. Genevieve icon painted by Howard Anderson

Allan works with a network of professional musicians, many of whom have become regular players for our Masses and events. However, every once in a while we like to add some violins to a Mass, and for homecoming Mass we always end with John Denver's "Back Home Again," for which I always like to have a banjo solo, and, judging by the reaction, so do the kids. We have had bagpipes play "Amazing Grace," and an accordion playing on one of our theme songs. Allan is able to write the music for any of the pieces we add to our little orchestra. Did I mention that Allan is Jewish? (Having the right people in the right places!)

My personal philosophy when it comes to Mass is not how often you go, but are you truly there when you do go? When students are forced into daily attendance, it may sound good to the traditionalists, but for the students, it can be an empty experience. I think that is why so many young people grow up and refuse to attend church when it becomes their own decision to make. It has always been my goal to have students feel that attending Mass is a rich experience, one in which they feel personally involved, one that inspires them.

The first day our visiting accreditation team arrived was a Sunday afternoon. We had classes in session. After the initial meetings and tour of the school, we invited the team into our gym, where our students and many of their families were gathered for Mass. It was Veteran's Day. We had invited the veterans who were members of our parish to attend this Mass to be honored. Prior to Mass beginning, we introduced each of the vets. Our students then sang a medley of the Armed Forces fight songs and each veteran was asked to stand when the appropriate song was sung. It was a beautiful tribute. We then welcomed our accreditation team visitors, introduced them, and celebrated a beautiful Mass together.

School on Sunday, Mass in the gym…it is who we are, and who we are is a community of God's children doing the best we know how to do.

"No other Catholic high school has such vibrant liturgies where everyone participates. It's unbelievable. It's really a grace."

—Cardinal Roger Mahony, September 2012

Making a Difference as a College Advisor

by Allan Paul Shatkin, Academic Counselor and College Advisor, St. Genevieve High School

When I first arrived at St. Genevieve High School in 2000, this once proud school had been dysfunctional for many years. One obvious consequence of the academic decay was that only a small percentage of the students were graduating, and an even smaller percentage were going on to college. I didn't come on board originally as the school's College Advisor, but when the teacher responsible for this post left our school, I asked the principal if I could

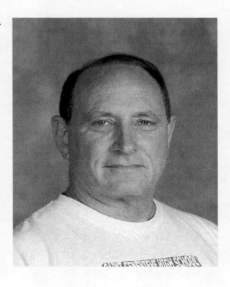

take over this role. By this time, I'd gotten to know our community well, and I believe that it is my knowledge of our students and their families that has been the main reason for the eventual success I've had in helping to raise our students' college admission rates.

St. Genevieve High School students fall primarily into three categories: immigrant youth, traditional minority youth, and first-generation American-born youth. For the most part, their parents never went to college in the U.S., and have little knowledge about the American educational system. They enrolled their children in a Catholic high school because a Catholic education was important to them — they didn't need to know more than that. I knew that to successfully move more of our students into four-year colleges, I would have to build relationships and trust with students and their parents while also helping to educate them.

One important reality I must always keep in mind is that most of my students live in two worlds: the "old country" from which their parents came, and current-day Los Angeles. So they spend their days in an American high school learning the importance of becoming an independent thinker, and then return home to cultures in which obeying one's parents is a value of far greater importance than independent thinking.

As College Advisor at St. Genevieve High School, I immediately understood that my challenge was far greater than simply helping my students plan for college. I knew that without their parents actively along on this preparatory journey with them, my students were going nowhere. They needed knowledgeable parents who could put aside their fears about their children leaving the safety of their homes to go away to college, parents who were not instantly mortified by the sticker price of a college education. My students needed the approval and financial support of their parents. They needed their parents to see them not simply as their children but also as young adults growing up in the U.S. So I set about putting together what developed into a comprehensive program of education, outreach, and confidence-building for both students and parents.

It's a long story, filled with many frustrating experiences watching controlling parents use every trick in the book to get their children to abandon their dreams of learning how to take care of themselves and become independent. I witnessed many fearful and worried parents do and say almost anything to thwart their children's aspirations to attend college. Some parents offered their teenagers bribes ("I'll buy you a new car if you stay home!") while others tried guilt trips ("Why do you want to leave us?"). The story is also filled with many very satisfying moments in which parents actually do see their children as young adults rather than as their "little girl" or "little boy" and recognize that they have to accommodate to changing times in a different country.

In the hope of helping other schools raise their four-year college/university admission rates, I'm including just a few of the key program techniques and tools that have helped me significantly raise ours:

- "I will be your College Advisor." When I am introduced at our school's Open House, (attended by families looking for a high school for their 8th-grade children), my first sentence to the crowd is always the same: "If your child attends St. Genevieve High School, I will be his or her College Advisor." Trying to choose a high school for one's child can feel like swimming in turbulent waters, and I believe that meeting the person who will help guide their children through high school on their journey to college is like throwing parents a life preserver they can grab onto and hold tightly.

- "I work for you 24/7." In that same introduction, I inform all prospective students and parents that I will be available to them 24/7. I pull out my cell phone rather dramatically, and tell everyone that they can call me any time — including Saturdays and Sundays, day or night. In the many years I have served as our school's College Advisor, I've received hundreds upon hundreds of legitimate calls requesting information and assistance but I have never had one "crank call." Rather, parents' and students' ability to contact me freely provides the same type of comfort as being able to reach a family physician when in need of one at night or on a weekend.

- Parent College Planning Workshops. I hold freshman, sophomore, and junior Parent College Planning workshops every September. Attendance is voluntary and every year our numbers have been increasing. Information about college expectations is shared and parents are asked to review their child's transcript (which is distributed, explained, and discussed at the meeting) to determine if students are on the right track. After each meeting, I always remain behind to talk with concerned parents. The goal of these meetings is parent empowerment. For the freshman workshop, it is also my first real chance to associate my students with their parents, shake hands, and begin in earnest to develop the relationships that will prove so vital in the coming years.

- National College Fair Attendance. I see preparation for college as a multi-year journey in which certain lessons need to be taught and re-taught in order to be fully understood and appreciated. That is why I take all our freshmen, sophomores, and juniors to the annual National College Fair held in Los Angeles. While the freshmen, even after being briefed, are not exactly sure what to do when faced with 160-180 college representatives, they do take home bags full of college literature, which helps to alert their parents early in the process that the effort to identify colleges is well underway. As sophomores, students become more serious; they start collecting information, and actually read and save it. By the time they are juniors, they know exactly what they have to do during the two hours they have access to all these college and university representatives. They get the most out of the experience (and they serve as great role models for their younger peers).

- Family College Planning Meetings. I try to meet with every junior family in my office for a direct planning session. If it is a two-parent family, I want both parents present. Because most parents work, I have made it a practice to arrange family college planning meetings on Saturdays and Sundays. These meetings are not about just providing information, but also about creating space for dialogue between students and their parents — so important because many of our families never really have a serious conversation about college. Parents and students often hide their true feelings about the coming big step. Many students don't want to say things that might upset their parents. Many parents operate through a lens of fear — fear about their child leaving home, and about the costs associated with attending college. It is critical for parents to know what their children's aspirations are relative to attending college, and for teenagers to understand what motivates their parents' thinking and decision-making. It is also important for these worried parents to understand their own motivations. When they have to face, in the neutral environment of my office and in the presence of someone they trust, that they may be preventing their child from fulfilling his or her legitimate aspirations because of unaddressed parental fears, there is the potential for real change. So these planning sessions are not only opportunities to provide information and talk about application strategies, they are also, in some sense, therapy sessions in which children and parents who, for a host of reasons, do not ordinarily discuss what is really on their minds and in their hearts, get the opportunity to do so. Being honest about thoughts and feelings never articulated can be both difficult and liberating. On average, these meetings run between one and two hours. Helping students and their parents appreciate one another's needs so that common ground can be found on the difficult issues associated with applying to and attending college cannot be neatly packaged into assembly-line 30-minute meetings.

- Keep College in the Air. I try to make a brief appearance on our morning TV announcements several times each week. There is always something new to tell students — some important deadlines coming up, some scholarship opportunity to share. With the cooperation of our faculty, I do my best to ensure that the topic of attending college is always in the air at St. Genevieve High School.

- College/University Representative Visits. We get frequent visits from college and university representatives. As our percentage of four-year college/university admissions has risen, so too has representatives' interest in visiting our school and meeting our students. I do my best to schedule these visits during our lunch period to maximize student attendance. When representatives visit while classes are in session, students must request permission from me in advance to attend the presentations. I keep a record of those who sign up and those who actually attend. I know where my students are in their academic progress and, on occasion, if I see that a representative's presentation is scheduled during a class that a particular student cannot really afford to miss, I talk with the student, and possibly with the teacher, and then help the student decide what is in his or her best long-term interest.

- Open Door Policy. If I am in my office, students just knock, and come on in. We meet during nutrition period, lunch period, and after school. If it is a question I can answer quickly, as many are, they leave with what they need. But if they are having a problem that cannot be solved with a short answer (e.g., stuck in the middle of an online application, confused about the FAFSA they are trying to complete, having trouble registering for the SAT), we make an appointment, preferably for the same day, and sit down together, often behind a computer, to attack the issue.

I am fully aware that my contribution to moving more of our graduates into four-year colleges and universities is only a small part of the larger and very exciting story about the educational experience that is St. Genevieve High School. With respect to the weighty responsibilities associated with serving as our school's College Advisor, I am grateful for the trust placed in me by our principal. I am also grateful to the many alumni who remain in touch with me after their graduations and who, four years later, invite me to attend the commencement exercises at which they will receive their undergraduate degrees.

Chapter 14: Somebody Help Us!

We were lucky. Though, of course, we didn't know it at the time.

In 1999, St. Genevieve High School was on the verge of collapse. When I walked through the hallways and corridors it felt like a dungeon. The lighting was dim, the furniture old, the flooring missing tiles, the windows mismatched, and the list went on. The location and "décor" of the principal's office were depressing, and since I'm someone who is very affected by my environment, one of the first things I did was to move the office. There were plenty of empty spaces for me to move into.

I say we were lucky because we ended up acquiring a couple of "godfathers" who looked after us financially.

Joe Rawlinson was the president and Ken Skinner the vice-president of the Fritz B. Burns Foundation. I had discovered that the foundation had a connection to the school because Fritz B. Burns, who had made his fortune in land development, was instrumental in building Panorama City, where our school was located. In fact, Mr. Burns was the one who sold the land to the archdiocese to build St. Genevieve Parish. The foundation had been giving money for tuition assistance and for endowment purposes over the years. But by the time I discovered all this, the deadline had passed for the 1999 grant proposal. I called to beg forgiveness, which was granted by Ken Skinner, who gave me a two-day reprieve.

Wish List

In May of 2000, after the money I'd requested had been granted, I immediately called to convey my gratitude, and invited Joe and Ken to come to lunch at the school with our pastor and me. The day of our lunch was extremely hot. The first floor of the school had no air conditioning, and we all had a good sweat during our lunch together.

During the luncheon, aside from noticing that we were in rather dire need of air-conditioning, Joe and Ken listened attentively as I described some of the positive changes in morale already reverberating among students, and happening at a somewhat slower pace among our staff. Fortunately, we had received a decent amount of press — local television news coverage as well as stories in the two major Los Angeles newspapers — about the good things that were now happening at the school. So I was able to present Joe and Ken with copies of the articles that had been written only a few months earlier, and give them an opportunity to see the news clips. Both men asked astute questions about what my vision was for the future of the school.

Shortly after their visit, Ken Skinner asked me to put together a wish list. He agreed that with the building in its current condition, it would be difficult to recruit families. He let me know that he and Joe were impressed by my vision, which, as was obvious to see during our luncheon, was shared by my co-administrators, who had joined us. Ken said that he and Joe were also impressed that even though I had been principal for less than a year, there had already been a dramatic change in the culture of the school, which was eloquently expressed by some members of our senior class who'd joined us at one point during the lunch.

Within the next several months I submitted my wish list and was promptly granted $560,000 by the Fritz B. Burns Foundation to make my wishes a reality. Ken Skinner personally delivered the good news to me. He also said, "Now that we've granted you this money, I want you to let other foundations know, and maybe they will help you as well." He even went so far as to bring Kathy Aikenhead, president of the William H. Hannon Foundation, to our school for a visit. Following that visit, the Hannon Foundation helped to fund a remodel of our science labs.

Ken knew what he was doing. Other foundations may have been loath to get involved with a school that was in such obvious trouble, and that had a history of dwindling enrollment. But alerting other foundations to the fact that we had received over half-a-million dollars from the Fritz B. Burns Foundation for renovations sent a message that not only had the cavalry arrived with much-needed supplies and there would be life after all, but that our school might be worth looking at as a place they might want to invest in as well.

The Vision to Succeed

Now let's get to the crux of the matter.

The fact is, Joe Rawlinson and Ken Skinner did not rally their board members just because they happened to be in a good mood the day they visited our school. In fact, I think they arrived somewhat skeptical, having heard negative stories about St. Gen's for years. Although the Burns Foundation did have a prior connection to the school, Joe and Ken were savvy businessmen who wanted to make certain the money they provided would be a good investment.

They were impressed with the story we had to tell, and the vision we had to articulate. Although it would be another two years before St. Genevieve High School earned a national title for character education, we were, at that point, well underway to achieving this goal. Every teacher and student who Joe and Ken met was able to articulate the importance of character education and tell stories from the past year as to how our character education curriculum had begun to turn the tide for the school.

What Keeps Me at this School

by Khristian Decastro, Student, St. Genevieve High School

I was very reluctant to attend St. Genevieve High School. I came here because it was my parents' will. All of my older sisters had graduated from St. Genevieve with a transformed attitude and mentality, but I did not understand what they'd enjoyed so much about this school until I enrolled and fully experienced it for myself. Though my parents had been very forceful in having me attend St. Genevieve, they had given me the choice of transferring if I decided I didn't like it.

Once I arrived, I chose to immerse myself in the environment that my sisters had loved so much, and I too experienced so much that was both beautiful and unexpected. I decided to stay at St. Genevieve High School for the full four years.

One of the reasons why I both attended and stayed was for the academics. I was accepted into an accelerated math program my freshman year, but enhancing my numerical problem-solving skills was only the beginning. My math teacher, whom I've had for all four years here, has become more like a close friend to me. Over the course of tedious bookwork and incessant practice, my teacher ensured that I got the help that I needed. Although I had a busy schedule, my math teacher always found a time for tutoring or reworked deadlines so that I would be able to learn and succeed no matter what. In fact, every teacher at St. Genevieve High School works this way. Each educator here is very personable; although they're authority figures, they also make it clear that they're here to assist in every way they can. They sacrifice their own time, during lunch or after school, just to tutor or help students with their work. The teachers are extremely dedicated to their students, which improves our ability to learn and creates strong relationships through which academics truly thrive. Results prove it, too. I have received a strong SAT score and passed all my AP exams, but only because my teachers worked as hard as I did so that I could reach these levels.

Outside the classroom, teachers and other staff members are equally as diligent. I've seen coaches treat their teams and clubs like their own families, and I speak from personal experience for the choir and musical programs at school. Like the teachers in the classrooms, the directors of these groups take the time to really bring forth students' talent and maximize our fullest potential. These extracurricular activities also present incredible opportunities that have made my decision to stay at St. Genevieve easy. For instance, every year of my high school career, I have performed for former President

Jimmy Carter. In 2009, I sang with the choir for his 85th birthday, and in 2012, we brought our entire production of *Carousel* — the whole cast and crew — all the way to Georgia to perform for him. Our choir also has sung in a benefit concert with Helen Reddy and even competed in Nashville in 2011. Having the opportunity to travel has also been very influential in my decision to stay at St. Genevieve. For example, our choir has performed for a convention in San Francisco and will perform soon in San Diego. Performing used to be a hobby, but St. Genevieve High School has extended this hobby into incomparable and unforgettable experiences.

When one of my sisters gave her valedictory speech at graduation, she mentioned how she would miss going down Roscoe Boulevard and eating at her usual after-school spots with her friends. These were what she called "the little things," the small details that make a huge impact, truly making this school a home. The environment of this school has probably been the most influential factor in keeping me at St. Genevieve. No matter who you are, you can tell that things are a little different here the second you walk onto campus. The simple energy of everyone's togetherness is amazing. It's the "good morning" greetings from fellow students whom I don't even know and the school coming together to sing with so much enthusiasm at Mass that keeps me here. It's the teachers becoming both educators and best friends, and the opportunities that come from performing with our choir and in our musicals. Ultimately, this four-year journey has been something I know I would never have been able to take at any other school. I've stayed here for the unique experiences that have been offered to me from only one place: St. Genevieve High School.

Do You Know What You're Asking For?

When Joe and Ken left our school that May day (pun intended!), they saw St. Genevieve as a rising star, not a sinking ship. In my mind, we were never going to fail. Once the vision of character education took hold in my brain, I never looked back. It never occurred to me that our school would fail. When we asked for help, it was always to provide something that would help move the school forward. That type of request is far more appealing to foundations and donors than requesting that they give to an SOS fund or pay off debts. These days, too many schools are crying for help. I've always wanted to be the school that asks for help so that we can better help ourselves in the future.

So why are you asking for help? Does your request sound appealing or needy? How will someone's help enable to you steer your school into the future, or are you asking for money simply to stay afloat? I've heard several school principals and even development directors sounding the alarm but not being able to point to a shore where they want to land their sinking ships. Saying that you can't make payroll or can't meet your bills is not something that most donors are inclined to support. If you can't meet payroll, why are you in business? Should you be? Instead of giving the impression that you need to be rescued, better to show that you merely need some help to get to the place you are already well on your way to reaching.

You may have noticed that this book is dedicated to the two men who believed in our vision all the way back in the year 2000. Although both men have since left this world, the legacies of Mr. Joseph Rawlinson and Mr. Ken Skinner live on in the work we do each day at St. Genevieve High School.

Chapter 15: From the Edge of Despair to the Cutting Edge of Curriculum

There are hundreds of Catholic schools across our nation right now that are feeling a sense of desperation. I've heard the term "on the edge" used dozens of times by worried teachers and administrators. "On the edge" is a phrase to describe how close you feel you are to closing your doors for good.

To move away from the edge, you absolutely must have the right people situated throughout your school. I can't stress this point enough. Everyone must be committed to making the necessary changes, taking the necessary risks, putting in the additional time, and most important, doing it all with a positive attitude. Someone needs to be brave enough to challenge the old guard, and the new guard, too, while also possibly nudging the pastor, cajoling the principal, and suggesting a change in the PTA leadership, wherever the obvious anchor lies.

Build Your Future

I'm not suggesting a big gossip session or picket signs or anything overly dramatic. What I am suggesting is that there be a businesslike approach to building a community that is excited about building the future. And it should be done in a way that is constructive, not divisive. That is why the Creating the Ideal Catholic School Community reflection included in Chapter

3 should be adapted and used with varying personnel when necessary.

Once you've assembled a largely supportive group of people, then it's time to be brave with your curriculum. What are some things that every child should know? What are some things that you all agree should be taught in schools but are not yet being taught in yours?

Considering how many of us in today's society are affected by divorce, which is compounded by what reality TV serves up on a regular basis, it's surprising that we don't have more classes on conflict resolution. Instead, popular culture is winning the day, with the person who screams the loudest or takes the first punch getting the highest ratings and their own spinoff show. Bad behavior is rewarded.

We know it is wrong, we have an opportunity to do something about it, yet we remain frozen in an "I'm afraid my school is going to close" mentality. Some call it survival mode, but instead of barely "surviving," we should be developing a relatively cost-free and cutting-edge curriculum in conflict resolution.

Once your teachers build their curriculum around something they're excited about, they'll "own" it, and the dynamics of your school will change almost overnight. Potential enrollee families touring your school will encounter engaged and excited teachers and students sharing stories of what recently happened during conflict resolution and other cutting-edge classes — stories they won't be hearing in any other school.

A Valiant Success Story: AP Calculus

by Taner Gulsoy, AP Calculus Teacher, St. Genevieve High School

This is my seventh year at St. Genevieve High School and my fifth year teaching AP Calculus. I am passionate about the subject matter and have attended several AP workshops to make sure that I can best serve the needs of my students. I'm proud of the fact that our hard work in the St. Genevieve math department has significantly raised the success rate of our students on the AP test.

For those of you who have never taken AP Calculus AB, the class deals with differentiation and integration concepts of elementary functions and their applications. On the AP test, the students earn a score ranging from 1 to 5, where scores from 3 to 5 are passing grades. When I took over the class in the 2008-2009 school year, our success rate on the test was below 40%, with the majority of those students passing the test receiving the minimum acceptable score of 3. Our numbers have improved significantly over the past two years. In

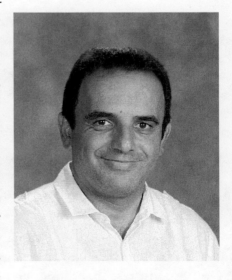

the 2010-2011 school year, 13 of our 16 AP Calculus AB students, or 81.25%, passed the test with a minimum score of 3 or better. In the 2011-2012 school year, 10 out of 12 students (83.3%) passed the test with a score of 3 or better. Not only have we doubled our success rate on the test, but our students are also getting higher passing grades. In 2011, six out of 13 students earned a score of 5, two earned a score of 4, and five earned a score of 3. In 2012, seven out of 10 students earned a score of 5, two earned a score of 4, and one earned a score of 3.

Extending these successes, last year we launched the AP Calculus BC class, which is designed for seniors who took the AP Calculus AB class during their junior year. All the students who took the class passed the AP test with the highest possible score of a 5.

How did we do it? There are many factors, but here, I believe, are the main points:

- **Early start**: We start teaching calculus toward the end of the second semester of the Honors Precalculus class. Students then take a summer component of the class where they get to work on multiple assignments.
- **Lesson plan**: We divide the concepts into units that introduce the theory along with examples. Students gain mastery of concepts with hands-on practice problems, working both individually and in small groups.
- **AP applications**: Once a unit is mastered, students work intensively on the AP multiple choice and free response test applications of that unit. This reinforces student skills and improves their familiarity with the test.

- **Review component**: The assessments given in class are cumulative, meaning students know that they may be asked questions from previous concepts learned at any time. Review is the critical part of every class. We generally finish our required material by the middle of February and have about two-and-a-half months to review the concepts. Students attend after-school review sessions in addition to class reviews.

- **Two practice AP tests**: The best way to prepare for the test is to take the test itself. We give two real AP tests before the actual test in May, one in the beginning of April and the other at the end of April. The tests are evaluated according to the College Board guidelines, and students earn a score ranging from 1 to 5. We then analyze the problems in class. Students feel more confident once they realize that they have succeeded on the tests, which in turn, improves their motivation and confidence and reduces their test anxiety.

Going forward, my goals are to increase the number of St. Genevieve students who are eligible to take the AP Calculus classes, and to raise our success rate to 100%. I have 100% confidence in my students, and believe that we can attain these goals in the near future.

How Committed Are You?

I always encourage our coaches to talk to parents about the importance of students' commitment to the team. Commitment. There's a word that has a powerful meaning, yet so few people honor it in today's world. I encourage the coaches to ask parents, "Have you ever had anyone in your life break an important commitment to you? Ever have someone really let you down in a way that dented your heart and your memory?" Unfortunately, most people will nod yes to these questions. Coaches can only help their student athletes realize the power of commitment if parents help them get to practice on time and make certain that students honor their commitments to their team.

At St. Genevieve, we challenge parents when they threaten to withhold their kids' participation in sports teams or other commitments as punishment. That's the wrong approach. We are becoming a commitment-phobic society. Beginning in elementary school (or before!), we must learn to honor our commitments to teams, school assignments, and family. We should be developing curriculum that helps students and families do just that.

For the last decade we've been reading about the rise in childhood obesity coupled with soaring rates of childhood diabetes. What are we educators doing about it? Some schools have banned soda machines from their campuses while at the same time eliminating physical education from the curriculum.

Let's Get Physical!

Physical education is one of the easiest curriculum issues to turn around — if you have teachers who are willing to make it happen. As I discussed in Chapter 1, it was my own experience with pancreatitis that inspired me to create our school-wide fitness program. I don't recommend anyone waiting for the same kind of inspiration.

Elect to Change

Earlier, as principal of St. Thomas the Apostle elementary school, I implemented what I termed an elective program for the students in 6th, 7th, and 8th grades. Typically, we had three teachers for those three grades. Each grade usually had 35 students. However, I realized that by being creative, I could lower class sizes significantly for the last hour of the day while still achieving daily objectives, unleashing a creative side of teachers, and motivating students.

So, during the last hour of every Monday through Thursday, there were eight teachers instead of three offering the following elective classes: Spanish, P.E., Guitar, Acting, Socratic Seminar, Jazz-Kwon-Do (a form of Taekwondo set to Jazz), Dance, and Public Speaking.

For one semester, students took four electives, one each day it was offered. For the second semester, they switched to the other four. By the time they graduated, they had taken three years of each elective.

Some might argue that I had to cut back on the students' language arts in order to make this happen. However, when students are taking an acting class, or a Socratic seminar, or Spanish for that matter, language arts is naturally infused into the curriculum, although the students weren't necessarily finishing the textbook, as some traditionalists would have preferred. But this was cutting-edge curriculum accomplishing objectives and standards in ways no textbook could come close to achieving.

St. Genevieve High School has been offering Mandarin for years. We even have AP Mandarin classes. We saw the need coming, we had the opportunity to meet the need, and we went for it.

On the other hand, although we have Smart Boards in several classrooms, we are not a school that currently offers large opportunities for technology. When it comes to implementing one-to-one technology, our teachers, by and large, don't feel it is time to do so, even though many other schools are saying it *is* time. I know I have a great and hard-working staff. So when they ask, "Are we wanting to implement one-to-one technology just to have it or to actually improve learning?" and we can't say that we're ready to use it to improve learning, then I know we're not ready.

My advice: make sure you have the right people in place and when they are excited to adopt something, then go for it. Being on the cutting edge means that whatever curriculum issue you choose to tackle, you're actually doing for a *reason*, not simply to *say* that you're doing it. It should be something that the staff embraces and values. It should be something to improve student learning and better meet the needs of students. When that occurs, you know you've moved that much further from the edge of despair and closer to the cutting edge of curriculum.

St. Genevieve High School was named to the
2013 Metro LA Top Workplaces list
by Workplace Dynamics

Made in the USA
Middletown, DE
09 October 2014